Reappraisals:
Lives less Ordinary

Rod Garner

First published in 2025
by Liverpool Hope University Press
Hope Park, L16 9JD

©Rod Garner 2025

All rights reserved. No part of this book may be reproduced or transmitted in any form or by any means, electronic or mechanical, including photocopying, recording, or by any information storage and retrieval system, without permission in writing from the publisher.

A catalogue record for this book is available from the British Library.

Cover imagery:
Emma Darwin (1808-1896)
Gordon Brown (1951-)
Robert Oppenheimer (1904-1967)
Samuel Beckett (1906-1989)

See page 163 image credits.

ISBN: 978-1-898749-24-0

*For Christine,
dearest and best.*

Books by the same author

The Big Questions: Believing with Heart and Mind (SPCK, 1995)

Facing the City: Urban Mission in the 21st Century (Epworth Press, 2004)

The Preacher's Companion (Contributor) (BRF, 2004)

Prayer: A Christian Companion (Contributor) (Epworth Press, 2006)

Like a Bottle in the Smoke: Meditations on Mystery (Epworth Press, 2006)

Beating the Traffic: Anglican Social Action on Prostitution Today (Contributor) (John Brown, 2007)

Crowded Canvas: Faith in the Making (Epworth Press, 2008)

Josephine Butler: A Guide to her Thought and Social Action (DLT, 2009)

On Being Saved: The Roots of Redemption (DLT, 2011)

How to be Wise: Growing in Discernment and Love (SPCK, 2013)

Teaching Virtue (Contributor) (Bloomsbury, 2014)

Something in the Air (Trinity Heritage, 2016)

Bright Evening Star: A Portrait of John Henry Newman (Liverpool Hope University Press, 2019)

News of Great Joy: The Church Times Christmas Collection (Contributor) (Canterbury Press, 2021)

Outsiders: Marching to a Different Drum (Liverpool Hope University Press, 2022)

The Print of The Nails: The Church Times Holy Week and Easter Collection (Contributor) (Canterbury Press, 2022)

VIII

" The realm of history is fertile and comprehensive; it embraces the whole moral world."

Friedrich Schiller, 1789

"Where is the Life we have lost in living?
Where is the wisdom we have lost in knowledge?
Where is the knowledge we have lost in information?"

T. S. Eliot, Choruses from 'The Rock', 1934

"The best moments in reading are when you come across something - a thought, a feeling, a way of looking at things - which you had thought special and particular to you. And now, here it is, set down by someone else, a person you have never met, someone even who is long dead, and it is as if a hand has come out, and taken yours."

Alan Bennett, English playwright (1934-)

Contents

Introduction 17

John Betjeman (1906-1984)
A poet and more 23

Clement Attlee (1883-1967)
The quiet reformer 29

Annie Dillard (1945-)
Alone again, naturally 33

Aleksandr Solzhenitsyn (1918-2008)
Prisoner of hope 37

W.H. Vanstone (1923-1999)
Wrestling with God 41

Emma Darwin (1808-1896)
"Everything that concerns you, concerns me" 47

Benjamin Disraeli (1804-1881)
The toast of the town 51

William Temple (1881-1944)
"The only half crown item in the sixpenny bazaar" 55

Nadine Gordimer (1923-2014)
"Say not the struggle naught availeth" 59

Samuel Beckett (1906-1989)
"Try again. Fail again. Fail better." 65

Karl Barth (1886-1968)
One man and Mozart 69

Kathleen Norris (1947-)
"Dakota: A Spiritual Geography" 73

Robert Oppenheimer (1904-1967)
The ethics of Armageddon 79

Adam Smith (1723-1790)
Money, markets and morals 83

Angela Burdett-Coutts (1814-1906)
"Seeing clearly with kind eyes" 87

Gordon Brown (1951-)
"Not Flash, Just Gordon" 93

James MacMillan, Karl Jenkins and John Tavener
"Towards the unknown region" 97

Vera Brittain (1893-1970)
The great cause of peace 101

Rowan Williams (1950-)
"It should not be forgotten" 105

Samuel Johnson (1709-1784)
To strive with difficulties and to conquer them 111

Willa Cather (1873-1947)
"The immense design of things" 115

Richard Nixon (1913-1994)
"Dick from the wrong side of town" 121

Blaise Pascal (1623-1662)
Scientist, saint and mystic 125

Denise Levertov (1923-1997)
Poetry, protest and pilgrimage 129

Reinhold Niebuhr (1892-1971)
Truth unvarnished 133

Thomas Hardy (1840-1928)
"Some blessed hope" 139

Stewart Headlam (1847-1924)
The roots of a radical 143

Charles Dickens (1812-1870)
"Much better to die, doing" 147

Thomas Müntzer (1489-1525)
The poor shall not be forgotten 151

Postscript
"Spiritual gold reserves" 155

Suggested Further Reading 159

Image Credits 163

Acknowledgements

This book represents my third collaboration with Liverpool Hope University as writer and Honorary Fellow.

My thanks go to Professor Atulya Nagar for his encouragement and Liverpool Hope University Press for publishing it. The task was eased by the good will and professional eye that Michelle Pryor brought to proof-reading and marketing, and the care that Ray Burns gave to presentation and design. Andy and Robert in the Reprographics Department also ensured that the book appeared ahead of schedule. My thanks to them too.

Some of the profiles in these pages first saw light in the *Church Times* and I am grateful for permission to reproduce them here in an expanded or revised form. Apart from my perennial interests and obsessions, they represent the fruits of conversations with colleagues, friends and students over the years who have valued learning as much as life itself. In such matters, I remain indebted to them, as I do to the insight of the writer Flaubert, that I still hold to from long ago: "Read in order to live."

Introduction

What is this book about? A fair and proper question for you to ask before parting with your cash on an unexamined purchase! At its simplest, what you have in your hand is a collection of profiles I have written in recent years that remain important to me. These short essays have stayed in my mind and their subjects help me to make sense of the very unsettled present. They bring into focus lives of considerable depth, complexity and achievement that shed light on how we live now and the possibilities of a better way of life. At one level this is a short and, hopefully, accessible read about ethics and moral clarity: what in the end might constitute a notable or authentic life beyond the acquisition of things, status and power?

Some of the lives considered here achieved fame and belong to the ages. Others distinguished themselves through their particular work or vocation, but remain largely unknown to the wider world. A handful invited infamy or hatred in their day, but history has looked upon them more kindly. The majority belong to what we carelessly and sometimes condescendingly refer to as the past; therein lies my second concern.

In a time of accelerated change and the bewildering immediacy of too much information, it is easy to become forgetful of even the recent past. Making time to pay serious attention to anything outside work, study, personal responsibilities and the need to relax, can be a struggle. In consequence, the contributions of those who have helped to shape who we are and the world we inhabit, cease to figure on our radar. The past is downplayed with the presumption that those who once inhabited it have nothing of interest or importance to teach us. Threats of cuts and closures in the history and classics department of our universities are no longer news. In a recent survey, one in seven adults thought that the Battle of Hastings was a fictional event. If history is off our agenda, if we have no reverse gear, there is the risk of denying the wisdom of continuity and making an idol of the present with its talent for novelty and the superficial.

In what follows, there are some significant dates that are worth noting and remembering. More importantly however, on view here are some unusual, even remarkable, human lives. In these pages, you will find much evidence of generosity, intelligence, and goodness, interspersed with instances of creative imagination, compassion and vision, which alert us to a world that for too many remains neither fair nor just. Just to be clear; this is not one more campaigning manifesto on behalf of neglected minorities or a burning earth. My aim is more modest: to introduce an array of characters who merit a reappraisal.

In short, a closer inspection, a second look or in some instances perhaps, a first acquaintance on our part, aligned with the readiness to dig a little deeper than usual. What they have in common is their ability to help us respond to a perplexing world that is not short of wonders. They can stop us thinking foolishly, shift our fixed, but actually rather shaky perspectives on any number of pressing issues, and make us a little less self-centred and therefore more open, to the immensities and hurts of other people's lives.

My long-standing love of words and reading means that writers and poets form a substantial part of these essays. But standing alongside them you will encounter reformers and revolutionaries, musicians and religious thinkers, prime ministers of high ideals and unconcealed ambitions, a disgraced US President with hidden depths, and a scientist who resolved to save the world through his genius, but was never quite sure whether he had instead provided the means of its final destruction. At the very least, this disarming band of pilgrims (I use the term loosely) would make excellent guests over dinner, guaranteeing a spirited conversation that would extend well beyond the morning light! Certainly, God and Christ, related matters of truth and beauty, suffering and ultimate meanings would shape their discourse, along with the perennial questions that have taxed the best minds for millennia. The philosopher, Immanuel Kant, summarised the task rather well: "What can we know? What ought we to do? What may we hope?"

If I may, I'll leave you with Kant's questions. I expect them to be around for a long time yet. As the philosopher Aristotle observed, humankind are meaning-seeking creatures. This inclination and need to understand - the unsatisfied and sometimes raging desire to transcend the limits of our closeted selves - sets us apart from all other sentient beings, however, beautiful and intelligent they often are. The emergence and predicted ascendancy of AI raises new and no less profound questions concerning human autonomy and uniqueness, but they are for another day and a different author.

Let me add just two more things. If you want to know more about anything I've written here, you can find a list of suggested Further Reading at the end of the book. Finally, as part of the community engagement philosophy reflecting the Christian values of Liverpool Hope University where I am a Visiting Fellow, all profits from the sale of this book will be donated to the Liverpool

Philharmonic 'Love Music: From the First Note' campaign that is helping to transform lives. This relatively new project supports its music education work with young people and children across Merseyside that provides rewarding opportunities for thousands of participants each year, through live performances, choirs, bursaries and the chance to learn an instrument.

Along with my friend and colleague, Philip Caton, I have been supporting this important activity for the past two years. This book will enable us to do more.

Rod Garner
Easter 2025

John Betjeman Statue created by Christoph Braun, 2012.

See page 163 image credits.

John Betjeman
(1906-1984)

A poet and more

Well before his death on 19th May, 1984, the poet John Betjeman already appeared to critics as a throwback to the nineteenth century. For some, he was a writer of exceedingly modest talents, prone to tiresome doggerel and a risible nostalgia for an England that no longer existed. Others were irked by his sermonising concern for the alleged destruction of its urban heritage or the parlous state of church buildings that, increasingly, comparatively few ever attended. Insiders noted that despite Betjeman's public persona of a dotty enthusiast clutching his precious teddy bear and sporting his trademark hat and mac, this affable mask concealed a reservoir of fear, envy, and guilt, fuelled by a precarious, if spoilt, childhood, academic failure at Oxford (despite repeated attempts to meet examination requirements), and marital infidelity.

Such personal attacks - in some instances, unfair and unfounded - failed to acknowledge Betjeman's talent and gifts. If he did pen embarrassing lines towards the end of his life when his muse and health were failing ('Blackbirds in City churchyards hail the dawn/ Charles and Diana on your wedding morn' come to mind), this is still the same poet championed by Philip Larkin, an acerbic versifier and critic, who notably lacked sentimentality: "Betjeman's poems would be something I should want to take with me if I were a soldier leaving England. I can't think of any other poet who has preserved so much of what I should want to remember."

Betjeman was a man of formidable energy. A genuine friend to countless people, a source of simple pleasure to the millions of ordinary readers and listeners who bought his poetry, and a generous and indefatigable supporter of conservation, who battled vigilantly against "institutionalised vandalism and the triumph of stupidity and greed over beauty". More than a poet, his roles as journalist, and radio and television writer and broadcaster made a significant contribution to modern culture, leading to a CBE, a knighthood, and the Poet Laureateship in 1972 (ironically, when his best work was already done).

Betjeman was a complex of contradictions. A retiring poet with a deep religious sensibility who was rather taken by Swinging London and its frothy celebrities. An outwardly accessible and often boisterous figure who relied on champagne and antidepressants to stave off an abiding melancholy. An aesthete who could be harsh in his estimation of the nation's propensity for ugliness and fecklessness - litter, pollution, and a general lack of civility or interest in matters spiritual - who also managed to be tender and revealing in poems that charted love affairs in tea shops, harvest festivals, and ladies' lavender sachets adorning the linen cupboard.

A devotee and servant of the Church of England, Betjeman was never slow to satirise or challenge its hypocrisies, vanities, and failings. Frequently troubled by doubts, he sought solace in the loveliness of its rituals and traditions, and the history of its parish churches where he "went to hear the old story told anew". In such places, symbolised by worship, the sound of bells and the importance of communities hallowed by time, faithfulness and continuity, he would share in the Eucharist that momentarily delivered him from an abiding fear of death instilled in him by the cruel and sadistic nanny who had forcibly fed him as a child, locked him in cupboards and spoke of the awful reality of "endlessness… and God's dread will". To face the "dreaded lonely journey into Eternity", he clung to the sacraments and the practice of prayer even as unbelief assailed him: "*I am the Resurrection and the Life*/Strong deep and painful, doubt inserts the knife." Nanny had done her job well - "I caught her terror then/I have it still."

Betjeman's deep attachment to the community spirit of the Church, its preservation of sacred spaces in which souls, love, language and civility might flourish, was not due simply to the understandable need for consolation that he desperately sought. It also reflected his belief that through Christian architecture, art, music and liturgy, a sense of a nation's living history and faith could be preserved along with the practice of social virtue, even in the face of indifference and unbelief: "And though for church we may not seem to care/It's deeply part of us. Thank God, it's there." Such concern was evident not only in his poetry, but also his many radio and television broadcasts. In his 1974 BBC film, *A Passion for Churches*, his carefully crafted words sought to reach an audience that "would include atheists and agnostics; Christians who had let their faith slip; people who loved the Church of England as part of English life and its churches as tabernacles of preserved history, without subscribing to its doctrines".

Far from appearing a cultural and religious dinosaur, as his detractors had implied, Betjeman now appears surprisingly prescient as we read of the emergence of 'cultural Christianity' and prominent atheists and secularists openly admitting their debt to a religion they had previously disparaged or denied. Richard Dawkins, Tom Holland, Jordan Peterson and Ayaan Hirsi Ali have all testified to the value of faith as a source of wisdom and meaning. In his recent and harrowing memoir *Knife*,

Salman Rushdie relives the murderous attempt on his life that brought him very close to death, and his subsequent miraculous survival. Reconsidering what he believes after such traumatic and life-changing events, he acknowledges how much he has been influenced by the Christian world of beautiful buildings, their music and melodies, hymns and voices and the depths of St Paul's letters and the Psalms. In each case "they have made their way deep into my being", even if he remains unable to accept the transcendent truths to which they point.

Betjeman would, I think, welcome such disclosures but with an important caveat. Christianity always represented for him more than a useful life boat when he was drowning and certainly more than an aesthetic fix or creative myth for public intellectuals belatedly seeking to make more sense of their lives. It was instead an arduous but legitimate way of struggle epitomised by the lives of estimable saints and scholars. A path in which faith, doubt and intermittent hope were properly grounded in the Church as "a living focus of love - God's love and ours for Him".

Clement Attlee. Unknown photographer, 1945
See page 163 image credits.

Clement Attlee
(1883-1967)

The quiet reformer

He was "a modest little man, with plenty to be modest about." Winston Churchill's description of his wartime deputy, and Labour Leader, Clement Attlee, reflected a widely held view of Attlee, even within his own party. Detractors portrayed him as 'a sheep in sheep's clothing', 'a poor little rabbit', 'an Arch-mediocrity', lacking charisma, hidden depths or intellectual substance. They were lampooning the decorated soldier who had been carried off the battlefield three times during the First World War; outwardly unremarkable, he made sure the country still functioned during a time of austerity and attrition before defeating Churchill by a massive majority at the 1945 General Election.

Unlike Churchill, Attlee never saw himself as a man of destiny or a political hero. He disliked the limelight, shunned publicity, and frequently proved frustratingly inscrutable to interviewers eagerly looking for the back story. He travelled Third Class on the train, often went unrecognised on the Tube, and refused an official car during election campaigns, choosing instead to be driven by his beloved wife Violet in an old, battered car. A special constable sat quietly in the back; Attlee occupied the front seat, briefcase on knee. Fifty five years after his death on the eighth of October, 1967, Attlee remains an enigma who gave little away and devoted himself instead to the lifelong job in hand: the arduous and unending pursuit of a more just social order.

To this endeavour, Attlee brought uncommon integrity, single-mindedness, and a practical intelligence: "The dreamer must keep his feet on the earth and the thinker must come out of his study." His principled pragmatism was shaped by early parental influence, socialist thinkers, and, from the age of twenty two, his residential work in the slums of East London. At Haileybury House, a club for working class boys that bore the name of his former college, he encountered the hunger, homeless children, infant mortality, and broken homes that poverty created. Making his way home one day, a young girl asked him where he was going. He replied that "he was going home for tea". In reply, she said that she was going home "to see if there was any tea".

In 1919, Attlee was elected Mayor of Stepney and three years later became the first Oxford graduate to represent the Labour Party as a Member of Parliament. In his election address he told his supporters "I stand for life against wealth… the right of every man, woman and child in the land to have the best life that can be provided…and the organisation of the country in the interest of all as a co-operative commonwealth." Significantly, such a future would be possible without recourse to violent revolution and would not forcibly purge the Establishment of its privileges. Enthusiasts cheered wildly, but for some this hardly represented the Promised Land.

Attlee's socialism owed little to Marx. He had been raised in a devout and principled Anglican family. Prayers were said each morning at breakfast and church attendance encouraged. The importance of humility and tolerance was emphasised, along with public service and the common good. Attlee respected the ethics, but formal worship and its accompanying 'mumbo jumbo' bored him. Wisdom resided elsewhere in the library of the House of Commons, where in between endless meetings and committees, he could be found browsing new books on philosophy and economics. He also found inspiration in the writings of William Morris, Thomas Carlyle and John Ruskin, and the poetry of Milton, Blake and Shelley. Critics would have been astonished to discover that Attlee's private library contained over three thousand books. At times he read voraciously - all of Edward Gibbon's monumental *The Decline and Fall of the Roman Empire* and Thucydides' *History of the Peloponnesian War*.

History played a part in Attlee's thinking concerning the question of the British Empire and the clamour from within its territories for independence. He had been educated at Haileybury College - a school in the Eton mould that had helped to fire his social conscience through its programmes at the Haileybury Club for working class boys in the East End, whilst also strengthening his patriotic sentiments. But while acknowledging the achievements of Britain's imperial past, Attlee accepted that the age of empire needed to be replaced by something better that represented more than cultural superiority and "a vulgar ambition for wealth". After 1945, and in the face of considerable political opposition, he set in train the granting of independence to India, Pakistan, Burma (Myanmar) and Ceylon (Sri Lanka), and the dissolution of the British mandates of Palestine and Transjordan.

On the home front, and against a backdrop of Britain facing near-bankruptcy after the war effort, Attlee led a radical reforming government that created the modern welfare state. Chief among its achievements was the creation of the National Health Service in 1948, and two years earlier, the National Insurance Act which required workers to pay an affordable premium, in return for a wide range of benefits covering pensions, sickness, unemployment and family allowance (child benefits). During its first year alone, the NHS treated over eight million dental patients and dispensed over five million pairs of spectacles. A politically daring contract was struck between the state and its citizens - a New Deal, as it was often represented - reflecting ideas and convictions concerning citizenship and commonwealth, rights and duties, that Attlee had formulated in the earliest part of his political career almost forty years before.

In keeping with his dislike of show and self-importance, Attlee's funeral service was a simple Anglican ceremony with just two hymns, 'Jerusalem' and 'To be a Pilgrim'. No press or television was present. Time magazine reported that "all trappings of power were absent". In 1979, a memorial statue of Attlee was unveiled in the House of Commons. At seven feet eight inches high, it stood three inches taller than the statue of Churchill which graced the Members' Lobby. A fitting riposte perhaps to the many who had previously underestimated or disparaged Attlee, and a deserved tribute to the incorruptibility of a great and principled Prime Minister.

Annie Dillard
(1945-)

Alone again, naturally

"Damn it; I'm going to do it, I am". The defiance is characteristic of the early writing of the distinguished American essayist and poet, Annie Dillard. The entry appears in a notebook in the late 1960s and reflects her determination to write a substantial book on the natural world. The genre was already dominated by male authors on nature, including the greats such as Thoreau, Emerson and Whitman, but Dillard wanted to do something different, however difficult. She wasn't a notable man living alone in the wild; she was an unknown college graduate student, married at the age of twenty to her former college poetry professor, and residing in the relatively peaceful suburbs of Virginia. A voracious reader, she had discovered *The Northern Farm*, a 1949 memoir by Henry Beston, recording an agricultural season in Maine. She disliked it but his musings changed her life. How could he not know, as she did, how fireflies made their light through the combination of two enzymes called luciferin and luciferase? She could do better.

By the time she came to write her book, Dillard had kept a diary that ran to over 20 volumes representing, in Thoreau's memorable phrase, 'a meteorological journal of the mind.' The assignment led to her working up to 16 hours a day, existing on coffee and Coca Cola, and losing 30 pounds in the process. *Pilgrim at Tinker Creek* was published in 1972. Literary fame came quickly along with a stream of invitations to write for Hollywood, model clothes for *Vogue* magazine, appear on television, and even host her own weekly show. The offers were declined: Dillard wanted people to read the book, regardless of her gender, age or appearance. In 1975, it won the Pulitzer Prize for Non-Fiction. Fifty years on, it is widely acknowledged as a classic of natural history autobiography.

The accolades were deserved, but potentially misleading. *Pilgrim at Tinker Creek* is at one level an absorbing and deeply felt account of Dillard's time alone in a valley of the Blue Ridge Mountains of Virginia. She lives by the side of the eponymous creek. The surrounding countryside is a familiar mix of cattle, farms, meadows, rabbits and rough pasture, but it is the creek that consumes her waking hours, her dreams and nightmares, and her diligent attention. She is not seeking epiphanies, but there are the moments when unsolicited glory bursts forth. The sight of a flock of starlings, an eclipse of the moon, or even a wild weasel enthrals her, as does the freefall of a mocking bird, and the rosy, complex light "that fills my kitchen at the end of these lengthening June days". What she sees and closely observes is touched with joy and a vivacity that relates a delight in simply being alive.

Along the way, she provides fascinating digressions into literature, philosophy, the natural sciences, and theology that reveal the breadth of her understanding. Scriptural allusions pepper her reflections and Mother Julian of Norwich, Gregory of Nyssa in the fourth century, and Pseudo-Dionysius in the sixth, are summoned to help her deal with the troubling question that represents the second half of the book. It is here that Dillard shifts gear, putting the goodness of creation to one side in order to confront the ubiquitous violence, needless pain, and death that exist within the particularity of her landscape. At this point her natural history begins to read more like the darker ruminations of Ecclesiastes or the unceasing protests of Job.

What besets her most is the irrefutable evidence of her eyes. As she observes a small green, frog with 'wide, dull eyes' barely four feet away, it begins to crumple and sag, shrinking before her like a collapsing football until only the remnants of his skin 'lay in floating folds like bright scum on top of the water', a grim testimony to the giant water bug that with just one poisonous bite, had reduced its body to a nutritious juice to be sucked out and consumed. Dillard witnesses similar ugly depredations on her walks and records them in unsettling detail. Hunger exists in the creek as well as beauty. Animals and insects must eat. In the process they devour their prey, their host, their offspring, their parents, and parts of themselves. Nature is complex, intricate, impossibly generous in its provision of species and forms, but also seemingly criminal in its wastefulness and indifference concerning their fate and welfare.

Dillard reels from this vision, at one point confessing "that I might have to reject the creek life unless I want to be utterly brutalized". It forces upon her the metaphysical question of how a creation so deformed by inherent cruelty, can simultaneously be the work of a divine and benevolent mind that has a care for everything that exists. The book of God, she discovers, is not easily reconciled with the raw book of Nature revealed by her forensic and insistent gaze. In the same breath however, she acknowledges that "the world is more than a brute game…and there seems to be such a thing as beauty, a grace wholly gratuitous".

As a chronicle of solitude and a meditation on all life on earth, *Pilgrim at Tinker Creek* shows Dillard at her most playful, questioning and fearless. She remains an essential and humane voice for those who find the natural world an astonishing sphere in which 'moments of vision come and go, but mostly go', leaving observers speechless in their train.

Aleksandr Solzhenitsyn
(1918-2008)

Prisoner of hope

Commenting on his death at the age of eighty nine on 3rd August, 2008, Aleksandr Solzhenitsyn's wife, Natalya, said that he had died as he had hoped to die: in the summer and at home. A peaceful end to a long life in which her husband had achieved international renown as a Soviet dissident and writer. Endowed with a prophetic voice rooted in the Christian faith, Solzhenitsyn's exposure of the horror and brutality of Stalin's prisons and labour camps was achieved in the face of formidable obstacles. Unlike millions of innocent Russians, who from the 1920s onwards had perished under the Soviet gulag system, he survived. Against medical odds, he overcame abdominal cancer, and later an attempt by the Russian secret police to poison him. Confronted by a labyrinthine and corrupt political system that depended on the efficacy of the lie in all its elaborate and distorted iterations to achieve its crazed ends, Solzhenitsyn documented the pitiless deeds that had led to unimaginable human suffering. Sent into exile in the West in 1974 after the publication of *The Gulag Archipelago*, and convinced that he would never return to Russia, twenty years later he would be welcomed back.

Solzhenitsyn's colossal book, running to more than fifteen hundred pages in its unabridged form, sold thirty million copies, discredited Communism in his homeland, and contributed to the eventual collapse of the Soviet empire. Distinguished commentators lauded him as 'the dominant writer of the twentieth century'. With the characteristic modesty that formed part of his complex and sometimes cantankerous character, he by contrast, depicted himself as "a little calf foolishly butting a mighty oak and thinking this could bring it down". The extraordinary fact remains that he did believe such an outcome was possible. Arrested as an 'Enemy of the People' in 1945, for disrespecting Stalin in a letter sent to a friend, Solzhenitsyn spent eight years in several labour camps, laying bricks, smelting metal in intense cold, wearing handcuffs for the slightest infractions, and hearing famished prisoners stealing his paltry food ration in the dark. By sheer act of will, he committed to remembering everything, including the unexpected moments of grace.

Receiving the Nobel Prize for Literature in 1970, Solzhenitsyn referenced a Russian proverb in his acceptance speech: 'One word of truth outweighs the whole world'. It expressed both the bitter experience of his subjugated people, and his belief that even the worst atrocities inflicted upon the innocent could not finally extinguish the human spirit. As a writer it was his duty to remind the world of monstrous things and how the lie had to be resisted.

Solzhenitsyn's years in exile, first in Germany, and then in comparative isolation in America, did little to endear him to his new hosts. Surprising students at Harvard in 1978, he inveighed against the West's crass materialism and barren soul, lamenting its "spiritual exhaustion" and its elevation of the human above everything else, including God. Against the expectations of the liberal democracies that had afforded him shelter as a potentially useful cold-war figurehead against the Kremlin, he remained alone and aloof, at heart still in love with his old country, if not its regime, and unimpressed by the empty enticements of liberalism. Set against the fate of the Russian peasants and Soviet citizens he still cared about, the prospect of being entertained to death in a culture defined by consumption and the mantra of material growth, simply held no appeal.

Opinions about him began to shift. Critics labelled him a crank or a has-been, and emphatically 'not the liberal we would like him to be'. Even in Russia, following his return, younger people in particular, came to view him, mistakenly, as a verbose commentator from the past, overtaken by history.

A deeper engagement with *The Gulag Archipelago* would have showed them that it was much more than a political diatribe or a judgemental tome denouncing human wickedness and the abuse of power. At many points, Solzhenitsyn reveals himself as a writer and historian capable of wit, irony, dark humour, and devastating honesty concerning the moral lapses of his own past. This, after all, is the voice of a former Marxist commander in the Red Army, who knew about its war crimes against German civilians - including the gang-rape of girls as a form of revenge for the Nazi atrocities committed in the Soviet Union.

In the labour camps that denied him the recurring duties and distractions of ordinary life that rarely leave time and space for serious self-examination, Solzhenitsyn confronted his own failings and transgressions. "I remember myself in my Captain's shoulder boards and the forward march of my battery through East Prussia, enshrouded in fire, and I say: 'So were we any better?'" This is the voice of a true penitent, who had renounced the Russian Orthodox faith of his upbringing in order to embrace Marxist atheism, but rediscovered Orthodox Christianity as a result of his experience in the camps. He was inspired by the prisoners alongside him: Protestants from the Baltic States; Catholics with rosaries, whose beads they had fashioned from chewed bits of bread; and the Jewish convert to Christianity who had once sat with him in the ward of a camp hospital and related the long story of his conversion. Solzhenitsyn awoke next morning to learn that his new friend was dead, "dealt eight blows on the skull with a plasterer's mallet while he still slept".

December 2023, marked the 50th anniversary of the publication of *The Gulag Archipelago* and provided a fresh opportunity to mark Solzhenitsyn's literary achievement and the moral and physical courage that preceded it. As a prophet who shunned mere denunciation and guarded against self-righteousness, he was not given to thinking he was better or wiser than others. What he did know beyond doubt, was the potential for evil that ran through every human heart; that we are therefore sometimes simply wrong, prone to get others wrong, and needlessly cruel. The corrosion that besets our best intentions is, however, tempered by what he describes as "the bridgehead of good" - the fortification that is equal to the enemies of virtue and truth. Solzhenitsyn's masterpiece still inspires. In the words of a beautiful, if piercing, Advent prayer, it encourages us 'to cast away the works of darkness and put on the armour of light'.

W. H. Vanstone
(1923-1999)

Wrestling with God

It was the practice of my theological college to invite a former student back after their first year in parish ministry to share their experiences with those about to be ordained. The speaker on this occasion that I now recall with particular clarity, had been well respected during his training. We paid careful attention as he recounted the rituals, routines, and challenges he had undertaken, and the personal cost involved. Concluding his talk, he recommended that if we managed to read only one work of serious theology in our coming year as deacons, it should be W. H. Vanstone's *Love's Endeavour, Love's Expense.*

After reading it, I wanted to learn more about its author. Against my hope or expectation, Vanstone agreed to act in a supervisory role as part of my post-ordination training. For my first assignment, I was to prepare a short paper on Jurgen Moltmann's influential book, *The Crucified God*. The appointed day came, civilities were exchanged, and then, sitting less than comfortably, I began, "Moltmann thinks…". Barely two words in, Vanstone interjected, "Mr Garner, I don't want to know what Moltmann thinks, I want to know what you think." There began a friendship that lasted until his death in 1999.

The obituaries recounted Vanstone's intellectual pedigree, First Class degrees from Oxford and Cambridge, followed by a hugely formative period of study under Paul Tillich at Union Theological Seminary, New York. Despite the outstanding gifts that pointed to a distinguished place in the academy or high office in the Church, Vanstone chose instead to serve parishes in the North West of England. This he did with uncommon personal discipline, and a deep commitment to the lives of ordinary people. He became a trusted person, who made time for the small talk that masked deeper issues, and provided an open door for the burdened or the sorrowful when their world went wrong.

As a host to friends and visitors, Vanstone was courteous, congenial, and frequently amusing. Decent sherry, strong cigarettes, and a talent for home cooking figured in his enthusiasms, along with the writings of the eighteenth century English writer, and moralist, Dr Samuel Johnson. Chief among his dislikes were superficiality, stupidity, and self-importance in all their forms within the Church of England. As a preacher, he prepared sermons meticulously and they were only ever preached once. Written as a specific 'offering' for each occasion of worship, they were then thrown away, their task completed. A serious heart attack ended his parish ministry in 1976. In his final sermon he told the congregation that "my heart has a lot to cope with at the moment. Please forgive me if I do not perform very well the last and most difficult task of leaving St. Thomas's".

A period of recuperation gave Vanstone the time and space to write about the issues that had long preoccupied him: the place and purpose of the Church and its ministry in a secular age; the need for popular Christian devotion to think again about the power of God in a theologically coherent way; in other words, to ponder the immense cost and struggle entailed in sustaining and redeeming the creation that Christianity proclaims as the work of divine love.

Love's Endeavour, Love's Expense, remains to this day the work of a writer under personal pressure, wrestling with the existential questions that are traceable to the book of Job, and presenting to the reader an image of God far removed from the One "who has the whole world in his hands". For Vanstone, God is not some inscrutable or imperious monarch detached from his handiwork, but One who is passionately involved in the laboured endeavour of integrating tragedy - that which has gone wrong - into the overall divine purpose. Divine control will not necessarily prevent earthquakes, floods, and cancers because that's the way a world with ragged edges is, but it will seek to redeem it. This is the hallmark of God's love. The world is not to be understood as a pleasing bauble in the hands of the Almighty. It is a costly, precarious thing that in its never-ending oscillation between the possibilities of triumph or tragedy, calls forth from God the unceasing commitment that requires us to see the Most High as a sufferer rather than an unconcerned spectator.

By way of analogy, Vanstone describes the self-giving of God in creation with an eye witness account of a surgeon performing an intricate and prolonged brain operation on a patient of great promise. The smallest mistake on the surgeon's part would have had fatal consequences. In the event, the operation was successful, but when it was completed "the nurse had to take him by the hand, and lead him from the operating theatre like a blind man or a little child".

The story, as Vanstone concedes, does not sit well with the Christian assertion that God in the absolute perfection and completeness of his own being should not be so affected by the world. But it is nevertheless, he insists, entirely compatible with the fact that Christianity also teaches that God, in Christ, has been crucified by the world. The anguished figure of Christ on the cross is therefore not a picture of God at one uncharacteristic moment in the past. It is instead a disclosure of a God who so loves his creation that for all time, the world, in its tragedy, sin, and suffering, and in its readiness to respond to or reject his love, bears upon him. Paradoxically, and not withstanding its proven capacity for self-absorption and shallowness, it is the "peculiar privilege and burden of the Church", as one small, yet also sanctified, part of the material order, to recognise itself and the universe as love's work. A love that lays itself open to manipulation, corrosion, and decay; that in its limitless expense, enfolds all that is, "even to the edge of doom".

Emma Darwin. Painted by George Richmond, 1840

See page 163 image credits.

Emma Darwin
(1808-1896)

"Everything that concerns you, concerns me"

In 1838, the idea of marriage seemed somewhat remote to Charles Darwin. Back in England from his long voyage of astonishing discoveries on the *Beagle* three years earlier, there was much work to do on the theories that would in 1859, bring him international acclaim as the author of *The Origin of Species*. A wife and children might prove impediments to his research and a sacrifice of precious time. On the other hand, he needed a home and someone who might be sufficiently interested in him to look after it. After careful thought - two columns of arguments, pros and cons, set down methodically on paper - he opted for marriage.

To his delight and surprise, his proposal to his first cousin, Emma Wedgwood, was accepted. Emma had previously turned down offers from several suitors. Intelligent, accomplished in music and languages, well-travelled, and robust in her opinions concerning artistic merit, politics, and religion, she cared little for kettles, pots and pans, and even less for a tidy and ordered household. Unlike Charles, whose father and grandfather were both agnostics, she came from a devout Unitarian family. As a freethinker, who had been raised to relish arguments, she was indifferent to Christian creeds and lengthy sermons. Her faith was grounded in a personal God, the necessity and efficacy of prayer, and a firm belief in an afterlife.

Almost from the beginning of their relationship, Emma became aware of Charles' lack of belief. It gave her some concern but never divided them. She came to love his transparent sincerity and the restless curiosity concerning the natural world that marked him as a seeker of truth. They married on 20th January, 1839. In marked contrast to the upheavals that would define their future life together, the service was a quiet affair. Charles believed that in Emma he had found a partner who would humanise him, and teach him there was "a greater happiness than holding theories and accumulating facts" or, for that matter, his inordinate enthusiasm for collecting and classifying beetles.

In a marriage that lasted over forty years until Charles' death in 1882, Emma taught him many things. In his own words, she became his "wise adviser". To this role, she brought a sharp mind and a dry, infectious humour that enriched their conversations and tolerated the nauseating smells from the endless scientific experiments that permeated the house: 'plants rotting in green slime, skinned birds and animals'. She even played the piano with a jar of worms on the lid so Charles could record their reactions to music. Emma proofread and corrected his manuscripts (Charles was a notoriously bad speller) and by way of helpful distraction from the treadmill of work, she introduced him to the pleasures of the theatre. When stress or pain threatened to overwhelm him, she provided guidance and reassurance.

Charles' debt to Emma was immense. Without her, he might have been, like his own brother Erasmus, a clever man who achieved little or an ambitious scientist thwarted by illness. From his early years, Charles had suffered from eczema, boils, palpitations, stomach pains, hysterical crying, and uncontrollable retching and vomiting attacks that often proved agonising and embarrassing. Emma was compassionate but clear-sighted in her care for him. She had to contend with other equally pressing priorities that bore down on her time and her own physical health. She suffered from persistent attacks of migraine and for sixteen years was continually pregnant, bearing ten children, the last when she was forty eight. Three died, including their eldest daughter Annie, who succumbed to tuberculosis at the age of ten. Her death, and the suffering that preceded it, proved devastating and confirmed Charles' doubts concerning a providential God. Emma found solace in the hope of heaven and the thought that Annie had been spared future pain. But her grief was palpable and for a while her faith was tested: writing to her sister Fanny, Emma confided "we have done little else but cry together and talk about our darling".

Despite the fact that all their surviving children also endured serious bouts of illness, they looked back on their earlier years as a time of happiness. For all the demands and difficulties of the household, they knew they were loved by their parents and remembered summers full of sunshine with "father lying on the grass under the row of lime trees humming with bees" and "mother dressed in lilac muslin wondering why the blackcaps did not sing the same song here as they did at Maer".

After Charles' death, Emma lived another fourteen years. Her mental alertness and range of interests made her stimulating company and she retained a youthful outlook. At eighty seven, she felt stronger than in previous years. In a letter to her daughter Etty, she wrote, "Life is not flat to me". She was reading Carlyle, taking a great interest in politics, dismissing the letters of Coleridge as "a mixture of gush and mawkish egotism and what seems like humbug" and sending letters of measured prose almost daily to her grandchildren.

Emma Darwin died peacefully, two days after reading Henry

James and Thomas Hardy. Like her wedding day, the funeral was a quiet affair. She was buried in the country churchyard in the family vault which had also been intended for Charles. He now lay in Westminster Abbey, beneath the statue of Sir Isaac Newton and surrounded by the tombs of the distinguished dead. Emma had never particularly cared for her legacy or reputation. Independent, energetic, and forthright to the end, she had favoured the quiet path of distinction and service. In so doing she enabled a Victorian scientist of frail disposition to formulate, according to the philosopher Daniel Dennett, "the single best idea anyone ever had".

Benjamin Disraeli
(1804-1881)

The toast of the town

In 1868, and after thirty years of wrestling the gnawing inward urge to make an indelible mark on the world, Benjamin Disraeli finally, in his own words, "climbed to the top of the greasy pole" and became Prime Minister. But not for long. Within a year he had lost a general election. The defeat left him disconsolate and depressed. It would be another four years before he resolved to secure the ultimate political prize again. As part of a speaking tour of North West England to promote the Tory Party as the truly national party of England, Disraeli came to Manchester on the evening of 2nd April, 1872. At the Free Trade Hall, and fortified by two bottles of white brandy, he spoke to a crowd of thousands and made his famous 'One Nation' speech. It lasted over three hours. After denouncing Gladstone's Party as a 'range of exhausted volcanoes', Disraeli promised a future in which public health, sanitation, decent factory conditions for the urban masses and food for the hungry, would take priority over the vested interests and *laissez-faire* ideology that defined the Industrial Revolution. The greatness of the country and the dignity of the poor demanded nothing less.

The speech was a great success: not everyone understood all of it, but the audience was dazzled. Disraeli's words and epigrams contributed to the pervasive and enduring myth of One Nation

Conservatism and its ideal of a fairer and more classless society. One hundred and fifty years later, Tory and Labour MPs continue to invoke his name as a source of inspiration. Speaking in Manchester in 2012, the Leader of the Opposition, Ed Miliband, pointed to where the Free Trade Hall used to stand and invited the gathering to remember Disraeli's vision of Britain "where dedication to the common cause courses through the veins of all and nobody feels left out".

The plaudits are to some extent justified but reflect the potency of the myth rather than the man. Disraeli was a Jew with a deep understanding of his own people and their legacy 'of all that is spiritual in our nature'. He was also a baptised, communicant member of the Church of England, who viewed Christianity as a natural successor to Judaism and an upholder of its ethical teachings. He recognised the plight of the poor and disenfranchised, and had read the reports of parliamentary commissions set up to examine the social conditions of the working classes. He had also seen at first-hand the misery and squalor of the manufacturing towns. In his influential novel, *Sybil, or, The Two Nations*, he describes a country defined by wealthy industrialists and the mass of the population who inhabit different planets and "between whom there is no intercourse and no sympathy". The book stirred social consciences and the phrase 'two nations' established itself as a telling metaphor for the 'hungry forties' of early Victorian Britain.

As a prolific and commercially successful writer, Disraeli gave voice to the despondent and brutalised multitudes. He spoke out against the police violence and harsh sentences inflicted on the Chartists who were demanding radical political change, and backed the Ten Hour Bill to reduce the working day in factories. Becoming Prime Minister for the second time in 1874, he fulfilled his promise of social improvement through a raft of measures successfully steered through Parliament. Some were advisory and others were ignored or several years in their fitful implementation.

By then, Disraeli was old, tired, and prone to increasing ill-health. He took a legitimate pride in the new laws, but his contribution to the drafting of legislation or debates in the Commons was negligible. Colleagues in the Cabinet noted his tendency to nod off in meetings when social reform shaped the agenda, and his utterances regarding the welfare of the underprivileged rarely exceeded polite concern. His private notebooks and letters over the years are filled with recollections of the famous and wealthy people he had met and worked with, and contain lavish descriptions of the 'dinners, diamonds and flowers' that constituted the fashionable parties he attended as a feted celebrity. It was a great thing to be 'the toast of the town'.

By contrast, poverty and the chronic diseases of the poor are rarely mentioned in his journals. It is also significant that he never actually used the phrase 'One Nation'. Disraeli's personal correspondence and, ironically, even *Sybil* itself, reveal his anti-democratic convictions. He believed 'that the fusion of manners, classes and peoples diminishes national and individual character' and argued instead for a renewed aristocracy and monarchy, presiding over a nation at greater ease with itself. Quite apart from the unrelenting personal ambition and egoism that lay behind his pursuit of power, it is conceivable that Disraeli believed that social reform really mattered in its own right to him, and to the party he led. He sought to alleviate poverty, but was not moved by it, did not, in Keats' memorable phrase, "feel it on the pulse". He was not for mass democracy or a classless society and resolved instead to revive and improve the old way of doing things, as a way of regaining momentum for the Conservatives.

Some critics, and even close friends, doubted Disraeli's personal integrity and questioned what, in the end, his fine words amounted to. After reading his final novel, *Endymion*, The Archbishop of Canterbury, Archibald Tait, was left with the disquieting impression that "the writer considers all political life as mere play and gambling". There is some truth in this observation. Politics was a great game for Disraeli. But to his admirers, his contribution to the common good represented a landmark in the social history of the nation.

William Temple
(1881-1944)

"The only half-crown item in the sixpenny bazaar"

In 1942, to wide acclaim within the Church of England and beyond, William Temple was appointed Archbishop of Canterbury. The prospect of his elevation, and his left-leaning politics, had caused concern in Conservative quarters; but the wartime Prime Minister, Winston Churchill, recognised his gifts and nominated him as "the only half-crown in the sixpenny bazaar". To his new post, Temple brought the formidable qualities that had already established him as a scholar, teacher, and bishop, and an acknowledged spiritual leader in touch with the sombre and anxious mood of the nation in a time of attrition. His reputation derived from his energy and vision; his critical intelligence and wide knowledge; and a deep personal devotion that combined with a sunny disposition and a capacity for laughter endeared him to many. It was hard to dislike a distinguished prelate from a privileged background with a Double First from Balliol, Oxford, who patently cared about the needs of ordinary people, and included among his passions a lifelong enthusiasm for strawberry jam - a truth attested to by his waistline. Wise beyond words in many ways, he was nevertheless surprised to learn of the existence of the Big Dipper roller coaster built in 1923 at the Pleasure Beach Resort in Blackpool.

Temple's time at Canterbury was all too brief, barely two and a half years before he died of a heart attack, aged sixty three, on

26th October, 1944. During this short period and well before, his mind had been turning to the future beyond the war and the urgent questions of social and economic reconstruction that lay ahead: what sort of nation was going to emerge? How would the poorest and unemployed fare? How would scarce resources be fairly distributed? Beyond the acquisition of credits and certificates, what role should education play in the creation of a purposeful life that also contributed to the wider good of society? And, no less importantly, there was a matter that had taxed him since the 1920s: what, ethically speaking, was the responsibility of the State towards its citizens, and to what end and purpose should the economy be managed and directed?

For Temple, hard thought on such issues was a religious imperative. In the darkest of times, he sought to provide a prophetic leadership informed by "service to the point of absolute devotion and complete sacrifice", centred on the divine life disclosed in Christ. From his commitment to the Incarnation, particularly as related in St John's gospel, he formulated the principles that underpinned his commitment to social reform throughout his episcopal ministry.

In the previous decades, first as Bishop of Manchester, and subsequently Archbishop of York, he convened and presided over major international conferences on the relationship between Church and society. In the General Strike of 1926, he mediated between miners and coal owners. Two years later, and, with many personal stories of human need arising out of his pastoral experience, he coined the term "welfare state" and began to formulate the Christian social principles that he believed should influence national public life. In 1938, under Temple's leadership, The Pilgrim Trust produced *Men Without Work*, a carefully documented Report on unemployment and its devastating impact on individual lives, families and local communities.

The publication in 1942 of his *Christianity and Social Order* brought Temple's life's work to a persuasive conclusion. Drawing on Christian teaching, he argued for the primary principle of the importance of persons and the necessary social and economic structures required for their flourishing in community with others. Citizens were children of God and deep in every one of them was "the spark of the divine fire". From this fundamental proposition he derived the three further principles that he listed under freedom, social fellowship and service. Too detailed to elaborate here, these guiding maxims or values could in turn provide a bridge or platform for more substantive discussion leading to detailed policies in, for example, the fields of education, housing, levels of income, and the necessity of work and leisure.

In this small and incisive book, Temple showed how it was possible to make connections between theology and the "giants of want, disease, ignorance, squalor, and idleness". In collaboration with representatives of other intellectual disciplines, he took the further radical step of drawing up a practicable programme - a road to recovery for a nation exhausted by war. Temple immersed himself in consultations with politicians, academics and policy makers. Experts in their field, they included the economist, John Maynard Keynes, the historian R.H. Tawney, the Labour politician, Stafford Cripps, who would later become Chancellor of the Exchequer in the Atlee Government, and the social scientist, William Beveridge, author of the unprecedented 1942 Report bearing his name, that would eventually make possible the provision of adequate social security by the State for all, from 'the cradle to the grave'.

Christianity and Social Order sold in excess of 139,000 copies and its reach beyond the Church made a significant contribution to the public conversation about common values and freedom. A meeting of The Industrial Christian Fellowship at the Albert Hall in October, 1942, at which Temple spoke, attracted ten thousand participants and included in its demands, 'a central planning for employment, housing, and social security'. Together with Beveridge and others he had enlisted in the writing of his Christian manifesto, Temple was preparing the way for a new post-war welfare state that he did not live to see.

His personal programme of social reform remains relevant to the vastly changed social order of today. The giants of poverty, health inequalities, inadequate housing, and glaring disparities in wealth, education and opportunity still remain to be slain. The challenge to the Church is to develop more thoroughly in our own time what Temple achieved in his, assisted by the same hope and clarity of purpose that defined his transformative labours.

Nadine Gordimer
(1923-2014)

"Say not the struggle naught availeth"

"I am a white South African radical - do not call me a liberal." This definitive statement was part of an interview given to the Times newspaper by Nadine Gordimer in 1974. It reflected the same clarity of purpose and self-understanding that informed much of her public speaking to global audiences, and the readers for whom she symbolised the conscience of a nation enduring the worst of times. Gordimer defined herself as a radical because she was committed to a world in which as her literary mentor, Dostoevsky, had insisted, "we are all responsible for all". From an early age she resolved that no one by virtue of race or colour should be denied the opportunities as well as the necessities of life. The world listened and accorded her a Nobel Prize in 1991, 15 honorary degrees (including one each from Oxford and Cambridge), and the Chevalier de la legion d'honneur - the highest French order of merit. In her own country, she faced hostile opposition and some of her major books were banned.

Born in Springs, a mining town outside Johannesburg on 20th November, 1923, to Jewish immigrant parents caught in an unhappy marriage, Gordimer's childhood was a mixture of simple pleasures - tea shops, soda fountains, Saturday matinees at the local cinema, trips to the beach - and an unquestioning adherence to the common creed of her white community that black people were naturally inferior, not clean and not to be hugged. Different in kind, they lived apart on the edge of town, huddled in an urban slum. Looking back, Gordimer described her early years as a "sad, confusing world in which to grow up and live in…where whites were afraid, resentful, and in denial". Her political awakening came through books and authors. Tolstoy, Chekhov, Proust, D. H. Lawrence, Edward Said, and especially her hero, Albert Camus, fired her moral imagination with their ideas concerning love, a shared humanity, and the role of a writer as a "responsible human being".

In 1945, after a desultory convent education, Gordimer went on to study literature at the University of the Witwatersrand in Johannesburg. Amidst a sea of white faces, she encountered a few black students who were wrestling with life's questions. From such discussions and the unease she had felt as a child passing the harsh compounds where black gold miners lived, her mind was set. A segregated, disenfranchised and powerless majority required more than sporadic blankets, food and medicine from the open hearts of white liberals who had closed their minds to everything else in a political system that required young blacks to call a white children's father, "Baas" and "Master". She left college without a degree, the same year as the National Party won a general election and implemented apartheid, mandating absolute separation of the races.

A brief first marriage in 1950 led to the birth of a daughter, Oriane. Her second marriage, just three years later to Reinhold Cassirer, an art dealer and refugee from Nazi Germany, lasted until his death in 2001. Their son, Hugo, was born in 1955. Gordimer's novels and short stories challenged the strictures and humiliations of apartheid, and imagined possible futures for a united nation beyond censorship and violence. As her international reputation grew, she refused generous invitations to settle permanently outside her own country. She joined the banned African National Congress (ANC), gave refuge to its fugitive leaders in her home, and lied concerning their whereabouts when authorities came knocking at her door.

A long struggle seemed unending. Along the way Gordimer witnessed and chronicled the hardships and hatreds that constituted the bitter fruits of apartheid. Promoting the work of neglected and banned black writers, she sought in her own writing to enter the world they inhabited, in order to understand their experience and reflect it clearly and unflinchingly so that her country could never feign innocence concerning its crimes. This was her "essential gesture" as a writer; to set down the truth, the reality of life, even when it conflicted with her own sympathies or those of friends and critics. Professing no religious faith, she saw godliness in a way that she could understand and respect in the courageous witness of Archbishops Trevor Huddleston and Desmond Tutu.

A turning point came in 1990 when the ANC was recognised as a legal opposition. Nelson Mandela was released from prison four years later. Gordimer was one of the first people he asked to see as the nation witnessed a new day. The liberation struggle was over, but poverty and unemployment, along with inadequate housing and education provision, still had to be addressed. A culture of corruption would also manifest itself under new black leadership in the form of greed, nepotism, and the abuse of trust at the highest levels of government. Gordimer had foreseen such eventualities in her writings. She was a realist: the human stain that Christianity traditionally described in terms of original sin was not the exclusive preserve of whites only.

In the years after apartheid became history, she campaigned against the spread of the HIV/AIDS in South Africa and the paltry amounts of money that went towards its prevention in a country where over four million had been infected: "If HIV budgets are relegated to a footnote, all we shall have left is a graveyard."

Gordimer died, aged ninety, in Johannesburg on 13th July, 2014. She left behind a body of work that constituted a social history of the nation and legitimised a human longing for a freedom that has yet to be fully accomplished and still leaves many black lives impoverished. No blame for this accrues to her. She saw herself as the keeper of a lighthouse. The analogy was not to be pressed too far however, and it would not necessarily "cast the beam of light that will save the individual, or the world from coming to grief on the rocks". Many prophets before and since would concur.

Samuel Beckett. Photograph taken by Roger Pic, 1977

See page 163 image credits.

Samuel Beckett
(1906-1989)

"Try again. Fail again. Fail better."

Since his death in 1989, Samuel Beckett's fame continues to rest on his plays, in particular *Waiting for Godot*. First performed in Paris in 1953, it remains one of the most significant plays of the twentieth century. It is a tragicomedy in two acts, in which nothing happens, except a frenzied and relentless conversation between two tramps, waiting for a stranger, (Godot) who never arrives. The play distils Beckett's bleak view of existence and exposes the emptiness and fears that attend human wanting and waiting. *Godot* is about killing time and clinging, however tenuously, to the belief that deliverance may be just around the corner. If not today, then perhaps tomorrow...

Beckett's friend and publisher, John Calder, described him as a writer searching for meaning in the world but "unable to come to any conclusion about purpose or believe in any creed". As an Irish Protestant, Beckett was familiar with the Bible and traces of it inform his work. St. Augustine was another influence: the first part of his famous aphorism "Do not despair - one of the thieves was saved; do not presume - one of the thieves was damned" found its way into Beckett's first novel *Molloy*. The Church however, held little appeal for him. He rejected "the very small God" of Christian worship, who took credit for the good things of life but "was never blamed for the multiple evils of the world". It is more than coincidence that Beckett began to formulate the idea behind

Godot after the Holocaust and the absent God who ostensibly permitted it.

In private, Beckett was courteous and compassionate, given to long silences, and revered by the actors who performed his plays. He was also generous and brave. In 1969, after winning the Nobel Prize for Literature, it is understood that he gave the prize money away to struggling writers. After joining the French Resistance during World War II, he received two awards for his efforts in fighting the German occupation. Some years earlier in Paris, he was stabbed and nearly killed by a man who approached him in the street for money. After recovering, Beckett visited his assailant in prison to ask him why he had attacked him. The man replied "Je ne sais pas, Monsieur."

Beckett's pessimism and antipathy towards religion have complex origins. He was born on Good Friday and never quite eluded its long shadow. At the age of fourteen, he went to the Portora Royal School before studying for his BA in European Languages at Trinity College Dublin. After relatively short spells lecturing in Paris and Dublin, he embarked upon a period of restless travel through Europe, writing poems and stories and doing casual work in order to get by. The lost souls he encountered lurk behind the characters in his later novels and plays - bewildered individuals just about surviving in a perplexing world. Beckett read widely, particularly the writings of the nineteenth century German philosopher, Schopenhauer, who depicted life as a perpetual swing "between pain and boredom". Buddhism also interested him with its insistence that all life was suffering that could only be diminished by the elimination of desire. Christianity by comparison, in its preaching and rituals, appeared verbose and insubstantial. Beckett saw part of his task to engage with "the questions the priests never raise" and to probe "where the human imagination quails or retreats".

In this respect, Beckett continues to represent a legitimate challenge to forms of Christian proclamation that rest on unexamined assumptions and the need for certainty, especially in dark times. As a child of Good Friday, he is sensitive to the often-unheeded cry of the maimed, confused and inarticulate, and refuses to despair in the face of the void or the prospect of extinction. Paradox surrounds him and this represents part of his importance for religion. Apparently convinced that life is meaningless, he writes poignant, honest, and darkly amusing works that suggest the opposite. And, as we noted earlier, he was prepared to risk his life to combat fascism. Unable to leave the question of God alone or deny the attested human capacity to endure and hope in the face of calamity, he treats his memorable characters with sympathy, inviting his audience to do the same. In his play, *Happy Days*, the central character, Winnie, is buried to her waist in a mound of earth that eventually threatens to engulf her completely. Despite the fact that she has little or nothing to feel happy about, no day passes without her trying to look her best and carry on.

Beckett is a secular 'man of sorrows', acquainted not only with grief, but the reality of a seemingly ineradicable evil within ourselves that we cannot overcome. In his voice, it is possible to hear intimations of original sin and the anguish of the first Good Friday - a world gone wrong when innocence was betrayed, friendship denied, and goodness excised from the earth. His plays lay bare the human predicament that preaching often fails to fathom or studiously ignores. Beckett's plays lack a Saviour figure but they serve as a terse and necessary reminder. If our gospel presumes to speak of the love and benevolence of God in a world polluted by innumerable ills, it must be *earthed* in the darkest areas of human life. However well meaning, cheap proclamation and facile sincerity are not enough.

Karl Barth
(1886-1968)

One man and Mozart

More than fifty years after his death on 10th December, 1968, the reputation of Karl Barth as probably the greatest Protestant theologian of the twentieth century, remains largely unquestioned. A Professor of Theology at the University of Basel for forty years, Barth's most ambitious work, the *Church Dogmatics*, was published in fourteen volumes between 1932 and 1967 and runs to more than eight thousand pages. As a monumental and searching exposition of the Christian message, it was later described by one reviewer as "a cosmos with no dead or isolated sections". In a time of crisis following the rise of Hitler, Barth was also a founder of the Confessing Church, emphasising the duty of resistance against the evil of the Nazis. In 1962, in recognition of his influence beyond the sphere of the academy and theology, he featured on the cover of *Time* magazine - a rare occurrence for a religious thinker. His faith was grounded in the Bible and the Jesus he encountered in what he called "the strange world of the New Testament". Indebted to the writings of St. Paul Augustine, Luther and Calvin, Barth was nevertheless clear that should he ever get to heaven, he would first ask about the composer who had always enthralled and inspired him.

Each morning after breakfast and the newspaper, and before his daily round of writing, lectures and meetings with students,

Barth listened to the music of Mozart. Along with theology it shaped his life, so much so that in Volume 3 of *Church Dogmatics*, Barth enlists Mozart as a conversation partner. In a speech at a Mozart festival in Basel, and addressing the composer personally, Barth said: "What I owe you is this: whenever I listen to your music, I feel led to the threshold of a world which is good and well-ordered in sunshine and thunderstorm, by day and by night." Other religious thinkers and leaders had come to similar conclusions, including the future Pope Benedict XV1. Writing in 1997 about his upbringing, the then Cardinal Joseph Ratzinger revealed that Mozart's music "still touches me very deeply, because it is so luminous and yet at the same time so deep. His music is by no means just entertainment; it contains the whole tragedy of human existence."

The remark goes some way to explaining why Barth, at an ecumenical meeting of bishops and theologians in 1968, and only months before his death, had suggested that the Roman Catholic Church should beatify Mozart. Like Ratzinger, Barth had come to Mozart early in life: "One day my father was playing a couple of bars from *The Magic Flute*. They went right through me and into me. I don't know how, and I thought 'That's it!" Whether singing arias with friends, playing a restrained viola in string quartets or listening intently to recordings, Barth's devotion and gratitude increased with the years along with his conviction that on earth Mozart had no equal.

It is a surprising claim made by a distinguished evangelical theologian on behalf of a musician, who was a Catholic, and a Freemason, not overly given to religious observance, and who, throughout his short life, as Mozart's letters reveal, retained a fondness for course humour and embarrassing bodily functions. None of this mattered to Barth: remarkably, he recognised in this unique and fallible composer something that had been denied to other great musicians and theologians. Mozart secured a place in Barth's theology because his music embraced 'real life in all its discord': its order, joy and beauty, and its shadow-side. It reflected the chaos, darkness and death that constitute the unresolved and anguished part of creation, but also pointed to a providential order in which "the Yea rings louder than the ever-present Nay". Mozart heard the harmony of creation and saw a 'light perpetual' that was brighter than the sun. A light in which Barth affirmed "the shadow is not darkness, deficiency is not defeat, sadness cannot become despair, trouble cannot degenerate into tragedy and infinite melancholy is not ultimately forced to claim undisputed sway". Mozart's music constituted in Barthian terms, a 'parable of the kingdom' - a 'Yes' to the creation that notwithstanding its shadow-side, "praises its Master and is therefore perfect". It disclosed the world as it is, in its incompleteness and raggedness; a world in which "life does not fear death but knows it well" because the Creator has revealed Himself in the crucifixion.

In so much of his writings, Barth defended the biblical belief that God could only be known through his gracious revelation in the inspired word of Scripture and the person of Christ. Confronted by Mozart's genius however, he comes close to acknowledging the legitimacy of a natural theology that sees evidence of God in sublime human creativity. Barth's endorsement of Mozart should not be seen as a contradiction in his theology. It reflects instead an aspect of his character: his ability, like Augustine before him, 'to think in questions'; his readiness to change his mind, to affirm, for example, in his later thinking, the humanity and suffering of God, as well as his majesty and otherness; and, not least, his requirement that theology should develop an 'eavesdropping' strategy that is always ready to learn from the world and other forms of humane enquiry and artistic achievement. By eavesdropping on Mozart in his early years, Barth eventually came to realise that God cannot be fully contained or entirely known within a theological system however elaborate or the pages of a holy book however inspired. Sometimes the mystery of the Most High is to be found in unexpected places: for Barth it was the end of *The Magic Flute*, where "the Yes rings stronger than the still existing No…and the rays of the sun dispel the night".

Such musical intimations of the sublime may have enabled Barth to live with not only the tensions in his theological writings, but also in his personal and married life. In 2017, intimate letters written by Barth, his wife Nelly, and his indispensable theological researcher, adviser and assistant, Charlotte von Kirschbaum, were released by Barth's children. The correspondence revealed a complicated relationship between the three individuals living in the same house and 'the deep, intense and overwhelming love' between Barth and von Kirschbaum. Despite the conflict between his marriage vows and the depths of his feelings for his colleague, who contributed massively to his professional achievements, a decision was made that the problem could not be solved by a separation on one or the other side. The relationship continued. When Charlotte died in 1975, Nelly organised her burial in the family tomb - the final resting place in which she herself was interred a year later.

Inevitably, the publication of the letters led some to criticise a love triangle that seemed at variance with Barth's theological ethics, especially in relation to marital fidelity. No further comment is required here except to note, as Barth himself taught, that reality has an anguished shadow-side that leaves no lives, not even the greatest, untouched. In such matters, the final judgement rests with God alone and we, in turn, can be grateful for the achievements, evangelical witness, and social concern that characterised all of Barth's life.

Kathleen Norris
(1947-)

"Dakota: A Spiritual Geography"

In 1969, Kathleen Norris arrived in New York with a dream of becoming a writer and poet. Fresh out of Bennington College, Vermont, where she had been a shy and bookish student, described unkindly (and, as Norris revealed later, incorrectly) by her freewheeling contemporaries as 'The Bennington Virgin', the move to the big city would prove exciting and unsettling. A job in arts administration opens the door to public poetry readings and literary receptions. Andy Warhol is sometimes in attendance. Five years later, following the death of her grandparents, Norris makes the surprising decision to move with her husband to South Dakota to live in the small house her forebears had built in 1923 in the isolated town of Lemmon, a community of 1600 souls. Colleagues in New York think she is mad but her heart is fixed.

Over the following twenty years as a freelance writer, and taking any work she can find, Norris becomes acclimatised to the limitations and values of prairie life and a physical environment that is desolate, unforgiving, silent and extreme. But in the emptiness and strange grandeur of "this great unpeopled landscape of earth and sky", she finds herself being changed. It is forming her spiritually and nurturing her craft as a writer.

The practical wisdom of farmers governed by the earth and climate, confronts her with the recurring facts of survival, suffering, death and renewal so easily masked by the noise, speed and consumerism of the frenetic urban life she has left behind. She is moved by the ancient religious traditions and hospitality of endangered Native American tribes. After ten years, and out of a felt need to rediscover the religious heritage of her Protestant childhood that she now realises has significantly shaped her life - "but for years I didn't know that" - she goes back to church. She also becomes an oblate (associate) of a Benedictine monastic community in North Dakota, and a frequent guest at various monasteries on the Great Plains. The silence that punctuates the liturgical rituals and manual labours of the monks sinks into her bones and she learns that the first word of St. Benedict's Rule is 'Listen'.

Norris proves an attentive learner. Worship and the wisdom of the past enable her to breathe and believe more deeply than she can ever recall. Her writing becomes a form of spiritual discipline, leading in 1993 to the publication of her bestselling book, *Dakota: A Spiritual Geography*. Part memoir, part spiritual journal and poetry, the Great Plains emerge from its pages as more than a desert defined only by the Black Hills and the Badlands. For Norris it is a place of disclosure and wonder. In its ostensible emptiness she observes Nature's astonishing profligacy as birds, grasses, flowers, animals and reptiles turn a dry void into a cornucopia of small, delicate and fascinating things. With the eye of a contemplative, she chronicles what Thoreau had described as our "need to witness our limits transcended" and recounts the experiences that reveal the stoicism, contradictions and richness of the ordinary lives that daily touch her own.

She portrays the frontier as a place where townsfolk are frequently forgotten, "viewed by the rest of the world as irrelevant or anachronistic". In this important respect they are, for her, rather like the Benedictine monks she encounters going about their prayers and tasks. But she also sees the desert making space for resilient faith, decency and kindness. It offers the possibilities of stability, community, and a settled place for the conduct of religion's proper business - that of becoming more human.

In the little town of Hope that boasts not much more than a gas station and a general store, Norris begins to attend the outwardly unremarkable Presbyterian church that bears its name. In time she accepts an invitation to become its unpaid lay pastor. She is nervous but follows the lectionary, stays close to the texts, and talks about the stories she finds there and how they might chime with the raw experience of the small congregation. Listeners are responsive to her promptings and she in turn is impressed by their generosity. The wider world of human need and misery exacts more than their intercessions. They are also realists, unsure of who will replace their ageing members, but content to "go on living graciously and thankfully, cultivating love". Desert wisdom has taught them that 'all flesh is grass', that institutions, however venerable, are also provisional, bowing eventually to the corrosion of time.

Worship at Hope is not a desiccated theological primer consisting of strange yet familiar doctrinal propositions. It is, for Norris, a communal act where "we gather together to sing some great hymns, reflect on our lives, hear some astonishing scriptures (and maybe a boring sermon; you take your chances), offer some prayers and receive a blessing".

Through her encounters with Benedictine wisdom and the vitality of a local church that is barely on the map, Norris discovers what is essential to her identity and survival: rootedness and silence; the value of the liturgical year; the reality of the Incarnation, and a living tradition - "a usable past" that is open to the future. To paraphrase a prescient comment of the philosopher Alasdair Macintyre, in a world that is always passing away and "the barbarians are already within the city gates", we are not entirely without hope. Some things remain precious and inviolate.

Robert Oppenheimer. Department of Energy, Office of Public Affairs. Circa 1944
See page 163 image credits.

Robert Oppenheimer
(1904-1967)

The ethics of Armageddon

In December, 1953, Robert Oppenheimer, the father of the world's first atomic bomb, arrived in London to deliver the BBC's annual Reith Lectures. The invitation recognised his international standing as one of the world's pre-eminent scientists. Less publicised was the range of his pursuits outside the laboratory: his serious study of oriental religions; philosophical enquiry; a love of literature, and the writing of poetry. Asked late in life by a Christian magazine, to name the ten books which had most inspired him, his list included the Bhagavad Gita, Dante's *The Divine Comedy*, and T. S. Eliot's *The Waste Land*.

As the Reith lectures progressed under the overall title of 'Science and the Common Understanding', Oppenheimer surprised his listeners. After initially reprising the achievements of Newton, Rutherford and Bohr, and the wave-particle duality at the heart of quantum mechanics, he went on to address the nature of human consciousness, the human community, and the "underlying profundities of the earth and our lives".

Oppenheimer's commitment to the common good owed much to the rigorous ethical framework of his formative years. Born into an affluent German-Jewish family on the Upper West Side of New York in 1904, he was raised in a culture that prized the 'high endeavours' of artistic beauty in all its forms, science, and public service. For his parents, the notion of duty, derived largely from their somewhat idiosyncratic reading of Kant's famous moral law, amounted to a religious obligation. It also represented their desire and determination to 'bring out the spiritual personality' of their gifted, if somewhat gauche son, who found other school children difficult and intimidated them with his knowledge: "Ask me a question in Latin, and I will answer you in Greek", he once remarked to a class mate.

The legacy of this upbringing was twofold: on the one hand, a man with astonishing reserves of intellect and energy and, on the other, a complicated, introspective genius, driven by a deep sense of public duty and a love of his country, that in a time of war would confront him with seemingly impossible moral choices. After Hiroshima and the unimaginable destruction that led to the deaths of more than 80,000 people, Oppenheimer never quite believed if he was the saviour or destroyer of an imperilled world.

Professing himself "heavy with misgiving", at no point did he ever concede that it had been wrong to build the bomb. He knew the Nazis were already building their own, and ultimately, in his view, it was the US President and his closest advisers who took the decision to drop it. In the aftermath, he acknowledged that "he had blood on his hands" and spoke frequently of his dismay at the escalation of the arms race that he believed, mistakenly, his scientific research would end. Asked more than once in public if he would do it again - participate that is, in the making of atomic weapons - he replied unequivocally "yes". His sin, he conceded, was not the human devastation that followed his ground-breaking work, but the sin of pride, of thinking that along with the gifted team of brilliant young physicists he had assembled around him, "they knew what was good for man". It left an indelible mark on many of them - in Oppenheimer's case, a deep sense of pathos and tragedy as he contemplated the human condition.

In his final years before his death from cancer at the age of sixty two, after a lifetime of heavy smoking, in 1967, he was invited to address an audience at the National Book Awards in New York. The surprising title of his presentation was 'The Added Cubit', an allusion to the Sermon on the Mount in which Jesus urges his listeners to resist needless worry and trust in God: 'Which of you by taking thought can add one cubit unto his stature?' (Matthew 6.27). Oppenheimer took issue with Christ's gentle admonition, insisting that we *should* take thought and *not* place our trust in fate, leaders or even divine providence: "By taking thought of our often grim responsibility, by knowing something of our profound and omnipresent imperfection…we may even find our way to put an end to the orgy, the killing and the brutality that is war."

A year later at another public gathering, Oppenheimer implored his audience that "most of all we should try to be experts in the worst about ourselves: we should not be astonished to find some evil there, that we find so readily abroad in others". He spoke as a man aware of his mortality and personal failings, who often seemed a mystery to himself. A close friend once described him as "a man put together of many bright shining splinters". A telling observation, but not all the splinters shone. Oppenheimer did have a genuine longing for friendship and affection, but he lacked the ability to form close ties with other people. His private papers running to 296 boxes of letters, drafts and manuscripts revealed very little of a personal or intimate nature concerning his family or wider circles. Some years after his death, his daughter, Toni, committed suicide at home. His son, Peter, worked as a carpenter and distanced himself from anything concerning his famous father and rarely made mention of him.

In facing his strengths and weaknesses, Oppenheimer spoke for all of us who value personal integrity and the need to face the deeper, more daunting truths about ourselves. He challenges us to heed with fresh eyes and understanding, the ancient story of the fabled garden in Genesis, where human pride and self-assertion have consequences that can only be redeemed by a Saviour. And in his insistence on the duty of hard thought concerning war and the threat of nuclear exchanges - prospects which dwarf by far the Armageddon of the closing chapters of Revelation - he reminds us that the fate and possible destruction of the earth is a responsibility that cannot be shirked. We are to wake from our slumbers.

Adam Smith

(1723-1790)

Money, markets and morals

Adam Smith was born on 16th June, 1723 at the family home in Kirkcaldy, near Edinburgh. He died sixty seven years later and was buried under a simple stone recording his name and his two great published works. Enthusiasts, including Margaret Thatcher, have hailed him as the greatest of economists, a staunch defender of free markets, and an equally fierce opponent of state intervention in economic matters. Critics continue to castigate him as the father of unfettered capitalism; a predatory 'wolf of Wall Street', ahead of his age, at ease on a frenzied trading floor where profit is everything and principles count for nothing. In the nineteenth century, the art critic and moralist, John Ruskin, summarised Smith's philosophy as: "Thou shalt hate the Lord thy God, damn his laws, and covet thy neighbour's goods." In 1936, Stephen Leacock, a Professor of Political Economy and humourist, was slightly more nuanced, expressing his accusation in verse:

Adam, Adam, Adam Smith

Listen what I charged you with!

Didn't you say in the class one day

That selfishness was bound to pay?

Of all your Doctrine, that was the Pith,

Wasn't it, wasn't it, wasn't it, Smith?

Both indictments miss the mark and, more importantly, do the accused a disservice. Smith did believe that self-interest was a fundamental and undeniable element in human motivation. In the book for which he is chiefly remembered, *The Wealth of Nations*, he wrote: "It is not from the benevolence of the butcher, the brewer or the baker that we expect our dinner, but from their regard to their own interest."

This conviction however, was not to be taken as an invitation to rampant selfishness as a guiding principle for life or commerce. Rather, it represented just one of the conclusions reached by Smith in a lifetime's enquiry concerning the nature, desires, and purposes of humanity. To this enterprise he brought patient and profound thought, moral clarity, an outwardly austere manner that concealed his generosity to others less fortunate, and a private life devoid of scandal or vice. He never married, had no love affairs or children, and remained devoted to his mother until her death, aged ninety. Opposed to slavery, he expressed contempt for those who in every age plundered, ruled and traded with no regard for the common good: "All for ourselves, and nothing for other people seems to have been the vile maxim of the masters of mankind."

Smith was also famously absent-minded. An acquaintance recorded in her diary that at breakfast one morning, he took a piece of bread and butter, rolled it round and round, put it into the teapot and poured water upon it before pouring it into a cup. On tasting it, he said "It was the worst cup of tea he had ever met with."

Following the award of a scholarship from Glasgow University, in June 1740, Smith travelled to Oxford University, where he remained for six years. Disappointed by the indolence of his professors and the exorbitant college fees, he devoted himself to English literature, ancient authors, learning French and Italian, and studying history. He read voraciously, acquainting himself with everything "that could illustrate the institutions, the manners, and the ideas of different ages and nations". It was here that Smith laid the philosophical foundations for his later thought, including *The Wealth of Nations* and, the equally important, if much less well-known, *The Theory of Moral Sentiments*, first published in 1759.

It is in the latter book, sometimes casually dismissed as Smith's 'other work', that he addresses perennial philosophical questions. Can there be universal moral principles? Does human nature change over time? By what processes, individual, familial or collective, do individuals become morally aware? Influenced by the wisdom and friendship of two outstanding mentors, Francis Hutcheson, his former Professor of Moral Philosophy at Glasgow University, and David Hume, the distinguished Scottish philosopher and essayist, Smith formulated his own 'science of man' - an evidence-based estimation of human life in all its aspects. He did this without resorting to the idea of some intrinsic and inviolate 'moral sense', as taught by Hutcheson, or fully endorsing Hume's sceptical view of the limitations of our moral capacities, forever thwarted, as Hume believed, by the controlling passion for self-gratification.

Smith thought better of human inclinations: "There are evidently some principles in man's nature, which interest him in the fortune of others, and render their happiness necessary to him…Of this kind is pity or compassion." Empathy or fellow feeling - the capacity to place ourselves mentally in the situation of those far different or removed from ourselves is, for Smith, the basic principle underpinning human nature. When we see others suffer, we suffer in our imagination. Conversely, when we see them happy and at ease, our imagination induces the same contentment and inspires us to look for ways to further it, both for them and ourselves. Smith invokes one more requirement, the perspective of what he describes as 'the impartial spectator', the ability or capacity 'to see ourselves as others see us'. Such seeing or recognition on our part approximates to a conversion of manners: "If we saw ourselves in the light in which others see us...a reformation would generally be unavoidable. We could not otherwise endure the sight."

This idea is all the more intriguing because it rests on Smith's observation that our individual moral judgements are to a great extent derived from looking at others. His theory proceeds not from the inside out, so to speak, but from the outside in. Because of the 'impartial spectator' and our capacity for sympathy, self-conscious moral introspection becomes a realisable goal that conduces to our own happiness and that of others. Without entirely discounting the possibilities of providence and divine assistance - Smith was, after all, a respectful Scottish Presbyterian - the business of being good and upright is a markedly human enterprise.

Any proper estimation of Smith should take into account his work as moral philosopher and economic genius. Both his great books merit serious attention and stand alongside each other without inherent contradiction. He did endorse the human pursuit of happiness, wealth and position, and the crucial role that trade and business played in people's lives. No less, however, he also insisted on the importance of caring for others, and the necessity of a helping hand if a nation was to flourish and the less fortunate were not to be left behind.

Angela Burdett-Coutts
(1814-1906)

"Seeing clearly with kind eyes"

By the age of twenty three, life had already been kind to Angela Burdett-Coutts. She was born in 1814 to Sir Francis Burdett, the first Radical MP for Westminster and Sophia Coutts, the daughter of Thomas Coutts, the Royal Banker. Tall and graceful with an endearing demeanour and enchanting voice, Angela was already a seasoned traveller, accomplished in three European languages, and blessed with an intellectual curiosity and steely will that belied her outward shyness. A welcome guest at society balls and parties, her future seemed assured, requiring only a suitable marriage and children by way of enhancement.

In 1837 however, just two months after Victoria had become Queen, Angela stood astonished with other family members in a subdued London room after learning that she had been left an inheritance of £1,800,000, equivalent to over £200 million today. This sudden and completely unexpected acquisition of enormous wealth, brought in its train an avalanche of begging letters, self-seeking admirers, and a questionable array of suitors.

Deeply religious and politically astute, Angela had other plans. Heeding her father's maxim that "great means demanded a great cause", she resolved that her fortune would do good to the many and not the few. It would embrace the relief of poverty and want; promote social work with prostitutes in London, estimated at that time around 80,000; improve children's education, and campaign for greater compassion towards animal welfare. Her Evangelical sympathies and simple faith led her to believe that in making such a profound commitment, the hand of God would guide her. The parable of the Good Shepherd was never far from her thoughts, and it would be her mission "to care for God's earth and beasts and people". She knew that she could not do everything to allay social evils, but she could do something. Her intimate friend, confidant and guide, the Duke of Wellington, endorsed such sentiments, but sought to dissuade her from projects that would be wasted on the most wretched and undeserving. She listened dutifully before determinedly going her own way.

At the outset, Angela directed her attention to the Church of England. She built churches in deprived areas to care for bodies as well as souls, and resourced schools and colleges with scholarships and endowments. She established the bishoprics of Adelaide, South Australia, and Cape Town to serve lonely and isolated emigrants who, with her financial help, had fled the slums of the burgeoning British cities. Aided by the indefatigable energy and administrative skills of Dickens, she set up Urania Cottage, a Home for prostitutes where compassion rather than condescension sought to restore their hope and dignity, and equip them for a better future. There were notable successes along with the inevitable failures. With Dickens' assistance, she became a pioneer in social housing: Columbia Square - four blocks containing one hundred and eighty apartments - was opened in the East End of London in 1862, providing space, light, ventilation, drainage, and laundry facilities to residents who had previously known only unimaginable squalor and the persistence of cholera. She fought disease in its various manifestations, supporting cancer research and helping to establish the Brompton Cancer Hospital (now The Royal Marsden).

The range of concerns made demands on more than her cheque book. She became personally involved in them, co-founding the London Society for the Prevention of Cruelty to Children in 1884, which became the NSPCC in 1889, and helping to establish the Royal Society for the Prevention of Cruelty to Animals (RSPCA). Although London remained the main focus of her outreach, other British cities were grateful for her support. Further afield, she gave generously to missionary and humanitarian work in Africa, Canada and Ireland. At home she received thousands of individual requests seeking financial help. She never travelled without a portable desk and many entries in her bank account were marked simply 'Donations.'

From time to time, she became exhausted by the task she had originally set herself and was prone to an underlying sadness evidenced in her later portraits. To escape she would go to Europe or, more frequently, Torquay, the most pleasing of her safe havens. There were other pleasurable diversions. She collected paintings, china, and rare manuscripts, and gave concerts at home. She always travelled in considerable comfort and wore embroidered silks of the finest quality. She had pet birds and animals that gave her great pleasure. Her parrots were legendary, one in particular amusing royal guests with the raucous insult of "What a shocking bad hat!"

In recognition of her unstinting work over many years, in 1871 Angela became the first woman to be made a Baroness in her own right. Ten years later at the age of sixty seven, she astonished and infuriated many by marrying a young American, William Bartlett, her trusted secretary and, at twenty nine, more than half her age. Queen Victoria was incandescent and presumed that Angela had lost her mind. She hadn't and not even Royal censure prevented the marriage that was to bring both partners much happiness. The decision to wed came, quite literally, with a staggering cost. Because she had married a foreign national, Angela had forfeited her right to her inheritance and for the rest of her life her wealth was severely diminished. The Queen never called at her home again. Undaunted, Angela continued to serve on influential committees and sustained an interest in the causes that had always mattered to her.

She died peacefully, aged ninety two, in 1906. More than twenty five thousand people filed past her coffin, paying their final respects to the woman they had affectionately called the 'Queen of the Poor'. Decades earlier, Dickens was perhaps more accurate when he had paid tribute to her peculiar and serviceable gift of "seeing clearly with kind eyes".

Gordon Brown. Photograph taken by Eddie Vanderwalt, 2007
See page 163 image credits.

Gordon Brown
(1951-)

"Not Flash, Just Gordon"

It was Gordon Brown's team who coined the phrase "Not Flash, Just Gordon" when he took over from Tony Blair as Prime Minister in 2007. The aim was to project the new man at Number 10. He would be different from his predecessor: less obsessed with public image, photo opportunities, and a 24/7 news cycle that never slept. Brown had waited seven years for this moment. He had already distinguished himself as the Chancellor of the Exchequer with 'the clunking iron fist' who had presided over the longest period of economic growth in British history. Now, in his first speech to the nation as Prime Minister, delivered without notes or the prop of a lectern, he promised to be strong in purpose and resolute in action. He would "meet the concerns and aspirations of our whole country…wage an unremitting battle against poverty" and reform the NHS. His brief remarks ended with his school's Latin motto, *Usque conabor* - "I will try my utmost."

There was good reason to believe him. From an early age, moral seriousness had been woven into his life and future ambitions by the example and abiding memory of his father, John Ebenezer. A church minister and pastor in the port town of Kirkcaldy, Fife, in the hard post-war years, he had worked tirelessly on behalf of his people in the midst of unemployment, material deprivation and homelessness. Poverty was everywhere, but so were the Ten Commandments and, seemingly, a church on every other corner.

Beggars at the door were never turned away and around the family table the children were taught to 'be grateful for what you have' and to remember 'it's remarkable what you can do without'. Gordon proved a clever and studious child, eventually gaining a place at Edinburgh University at the age of sixteen.

Learning was important, but he loved sport even more. For every half hour of homework there was an hour kicking a football in the garden. He found it hard to understand why his father applauded good play on both sides when he took him to watch Raith Rovers. Later he grasped that it was all about fairness and respect.

Sport was almost the boy's undoing. During Gordon's last rugby match at school, he was kicked in the head and became permanently blind in one eye. Surgery five years later saved his second eye. Throughout his political career, documents had to be prepared in very large type. His visual limitations never impeded his ambitions, and in some measure would shape his political character, including the awareness that others frequently faced difficulties far worse than his own.

Undoubtedly, this perspective (formed by wide reading as well as family upbringing) helped Brown in 2010 when he conceded that his opportunity as Prime Minister to fulfil his promise to the people was to be short-lived. His tenure ended with the onset of a decade of austerity, compounded by the 2008 financial crash and the belief on his part that voters had grown tired of a Labour Government. In addition, many had not forgotten or forgiven its disastrous intervention in the Iraq War in 2003. Electoral defeat was followed by the collapse of Brown's economic legacy. There had been significant achievements during his brief occupation of the highest office of State, notably (and now largely forgotten) his successful organising of an international response to the crash. Travelling tens of thousands of miles across the globe in rapid succession in order to concentrate the minds of leaders that mattered, he brought them together to agree a strategy at the London G20 summit in April, 2009. The plaudits were loud and sincere in recognition of the man 'who may have saved the world from a second great depression'.

In the spirit of his old school motto, Brown had done his best. But even this global achievement could not mitigate the crushing disappointment of the ballot box result that would follow a year later. In defeat, he accepted personal responsibility and, privately, felt that he had let millions of people down. Unable to form a majority in the House of Commons, he resigned. In his resignation speech he reiterated that he had 'loved the job, not for its prestige, its titles and its ceremony…but "for its potential to make this country I love fairer, more tolerant, more green…more prosperous and more just". Accompanied by his wife Sarah, and children, John and Fraser, they left Downing Street for the last time, walking quietly 'into the suddenly gathering twilight'.

The poignancy of the scene seems to confirm that a political career of considerable distinction had ended in failure. In one obvious respect of course - rejection at the hands of the electorate - it had. But as he approached sixty, it was not to prove the end of Brown's laudable ambition to make a difference or his extraordinary capacity for work. Unlike some of his predecessors - and one or two who came afterwards who made fortunes from stupidly lucrative lecture tours and multiple board room appointments - Brown initially took time to reconsider his priorities, including his important role as a father and husband. It would be seven years before he published his memoirs. In the meantime, he continued with his constituency work as an MP and served as the United Nation's special envoy for global education. Employing a small team led by a highly-qualified education expert, the role took him to countries where millions of children had no access to learning, including Pakistan, India, South Sudan, Uganda, Jordan, Lebanon and Turkey. The work was funded by the proceeds of his public speaking and writing that were also donated to his other charitable causes. Four years after leaving Downing Street, when Scotland seemed to be reaching towards independence, Brown also became a prominent voice in the fevered national debate. Addressing a gathering of pro-union campaigners, exhausted by weeks of abuse and being told they were counterfeit Scots, Brown, visibly shaking with intensity, compelled them to hold their heads high: "Let us tell the nationalists this is not their flag, their country, their culture, their streets." This was the voice of a public servant, who for forty years had repeatedly demonstrated his commitment to the unity and integrity of Britain. A voice that was drowned as his speech ended by the rapturous applause of his listeners in the deprived Maryhill district of Glasgow. A reminder, as one reviewer of Brown's autobiography pointed out, that despite his setbacks and mistakes as Prime Minister, 'when he was good, he was very good indeed'. Very good that is in terms of his fundamental decency and political talents. Both continue to make an important and compassionate contribution to the national and global conversation concerning the environment, human dignity and child poverty.

James MacMillan, Karl Jenkins and John Tavener

"Towards the unknown region"

Sir James MacMillan celebrated his sixty fifth birthday on 16th July, 2024, just three days before the opening of the annual Proms Season. The pre-eminent Scottish composer of his generation, MacMillan first attracted critical acclaim with his celebrated Proms premiere of *The Confession of Isobel Gowdie* in 1990. Since then, his interest in deep theological and philosophical issues rooted in a questioning and robust Catholic faith, has led to symphonies, operas, and choral works performed by the world's best orchestras and choirs.

Two other distinguished composers whose musical creativity owes much to Christianity have also recently recorded important anniversaries. Sir Karl Jenkins, marked his 80th birthday in February 2024. The son of a Welsh Methodist father and teacher who played the chapel organ, Jenkins is widely regarded as one of the world's most performed living composers. Crossing cultural and spiritual boundaries and often using ancient instruments, he draws on the texts and ideas of diverse religious and musical traditions to reach those who are not religious, yet find solace and purpose in his concerts and recordings.

Across the Welsh border, Sir John Tavener, who died in 2013, was born in London to Presbyterian parents eighty one years ago on 28th January, 1944. Managing the demands of a family building firm, they gave their talented son a religious upbringing and nurtured his musical gifts. In the 1970s, Tavener turned to the spirituality of the Orthodox Church for inspiration. Public recognition came in 1989 with *The Protecting Veil* - a devotional work for cello and strings that many now regard as his masterpiece. First performed at the BBC Proms that year, in Tavener's words, it seeks to capture the beauty, pathos, and 'some of the almost cosmic power of the Mother of God'. Labelled carelessly as a 'holy minimalist' by his detractors, the growing appeal of his music defied critical opinion. Global celebrity followed in 1997, when his *Song for Athene* concluded the funeral service for Diana, Princess of Wales.

In a culture still disposed to find talk about God difficult, to the point of embarrassment, the music of MacMillan, Jenkins and Tavener constitutes an unfashionable wager on the reality of divine transcendence. Underpinning their work is the uncommon assumption of God's presence, a reaching out towards the ineffable beyond ordinary speech or images, and a desire for some ultimate source of union, peace and healing. Taking metaphysics seriously, they engage listeners in the mystery of existence, the necessity and value of silence, and the challenge of learning again what it is to be human in a world where intimations of joy, hope, and heaven exist uneasily, alongside suffering and a felt absence of meaning.

Like many other esteemed composers, MacMillan believes that music begins in silence. From his personal experience, he has testified that it can also emerge out of grief. In January 2016, his granddaughter, Sara Maria, died shortly before her sixth birthday. Born with a congenital brain condition, she was blind, partially deaf and immobile. At the Requiem Mass in Glasgow, MacMillan delivered a moving eulogy on the inestimable worth of every human life, especially those with special needs. During the service, members of the Cappa Novella choir performed his composition *Think of how God Loves you*:

Think of how God loves you!

He calls you his own children.

and that is what you are.

You have put on Christ;

In him you have been baptised. Alleluia!

MacMillan dedicated this tender choral piece to Sara Maria. For him, she was there in the music: "a very damaged wee girl who brought tremendous joy, and I would say religious understanding, to her mother, and to the rest of us too". Within weeks of her death, he was back at his desk composing, aware that something had changed - a change to which his music gave voice. A small, broken child had opened up to him "the *essence* of human life" beyond power, money or influence. Suffering had been given a shape in his music and transformed into something beautiful.

In his recent work for soloists, chorus and orchestra, *One World*, Karl Jenkins sets out a utopian vision of a future world restored "under the kingdom of God". The early movements acknowledge its current parlous state, the long search of humanity for a form of happiness and fulfilment beyond dogmas and creeds, and the Hebraic duty of *Tikkun Olam* - the task of 'repairing the world' by attending to its hurts and injustices. They reflect Jenkins's personal *credo*: a way of seeing the world, traceable in part to the death of his mother when he was aged five, and the residual Calvinism of his Methodist upbringing with its dark and juridical prospect of a hereafter. As a 'composer of peace' who is 'essentially Christian', his music honours the cries of children and the weeping of mothers caught in the blast of war. Beyond the exercise of human compassion, it asks for divine mercy and redemption, a final healing in a universal afterlife more mysterious and capacious than the traditional heaven of the chosen and the blessed.

Jenkins's mysticism finds its counterpart in the later works of Tavener. Following a diagnosis with Marfan Syndrome, a hereditary condition affecting the connective tissue, and never entirely well after an earlier stroke, his musical vision extended beyond the confines of the Orthodox faith that had once felt like a 'homecoming', to embrace a more universalist philosophy. His devotion to the Virgin Mary remained, but his Requiem in 2008 for cello, soloists, chorus and orchestra ventured further. Premiered in The Metropolitan Cathedral of Christ the King, Liverpool, it contained texts from the Catholic liturgy, Sufi poetry, the Koran, and the Upanishads. Explaining their inclusion, Tavener commented that the heart and meaning of the Requiem was to be found in the words "Our glory lies where we cease to exist." In keeping with some of his earlier works it was essentially about a journey and becoming "one with God". If this did not amount to a comprehensive or definitive creed for listeners wanting certainty in matters of believing, it served as an important reminder of the mystical strand within Christianity: the hidden and overlooked stream that has helped to shape its history.

Vera Brittain
(1893-1970)

The great cause of peace

Shortly before midnight on 16th February, 1933, Vera Brittain finished the final sentences of *Testament of Youth*. It represented the fulfilment of her long-standing resolve to immortalise in a personal memoir the story of her generation - the women and men who grew up just before 1914 and the Great War. She wanted it to be a truthful and abiding elegy for the dead, and, above all, an indictment of modern warfare and its legacy of suffering and grief. The book was inscribed with verses from Ecclesiasticus: 'And some there be, which have no memorial; who are perished, as though they had never been; and are become as though they had never been born…The people will tell of their wisdom, and the congregation will show forth their praise'. (44. vv 9.15).

It took her three years of toil - disciplined hours, carved out of a crowded daily schedule that included managing a household, caring for her family, and campaigning vigorously for peace and women's rights. At thirty nine, she was married to a political scientist, George Caitlin, and the mother of two children. Her relationship with John would always prove difficult; Shirley would eventually become a Labour Cabinet Minister. The book completed, there remained only the daunting question of how it would be received by her publisher. The reply came five days later. It read:

"Dear Miss Brittain,

I have read Testament of Youth with the greatest admiration. It is a book of great beauty, and even greater courage, and I shall be very pleased to publish it. In places, I confess, it moved me intolerably."

Readers and critics came to the same conclusion. Virginia Woolf stayed up all night to finish it. *The New York Times* reviewer described it as "hauntingly beautiful". There were a few carping critics, but by the end of the decade, it had sold 120,000 copies.

Its emotional impact owed much to Brittain's personal history. As war broke out in 1914, she had already gained a place at Oxford to read English. What appeared at first to be a temporary lull in her ambition to pursue a literary career, soon changed her life completely. Unashamedly patriotic, and inspired by a sermon from the Bishop of Oxford to uphold the nation's 'righteous and honourable ideals' so that soldiers might feel England was worth fighting for, she deferred her studies and dedicated herself to nursing the wounded and dying.

For the next four years she worked at hospitals in London, Malta and Northern France. Routine domestic duties sat alongside twelve hour shifts, often without a break, as she coped with the 'butcher's shop' - bodies that had been gassed, burned, and maimed. Grotesque wounds could overwhelm even the most experienced and professional nurses, but there was little time for pity or tears. She was expected to carry on, appearing "punctually on duty looking clean, tidy and cheerful". During the same period, the war took from her the four people she had loved most: her fiancé, Roland, her brother, Edward, and two of her closest male friends.

By the end of the war, Brittain was exhausted and still consumed by grief. Disillusioned by the terrible human cost of conflict, it was only a fierce ambition that enabled her to hold on to life. Returning to Oxford, she pursued her calling to be a writer. Graduation was made possible with the aid of a large dose of brandy before she faced the examiners. An extended holiday in France and Italy proved restorative, after which she returned to England to establish a career as a freelance journalist, novelist, and campaigner.

She joined the Labour Party and the increasingly influential League of Nations Union, formed in 1918, to promote collective security and permanent peace between countries. She had travelled extensively through Europe and found distressing evidence of hunger, humiliation, hatred and fear. Words from the book of Ecclesiastes spoke to her experiences: 'So I returned, and considered all the oppressions that are done under the sun: and behold the tears of such as were oppressed, and they had no comforter' (4 v.1).

What Brittain had witnessed marked the beginning of her journey towards the radical pacifism that would immerse her in international lecture tours, large peace rallies, and fundraising for food relief on behalf of the Peace Pledge Union. She spoke out uncompromisingly against the saturation bombing of German cities and was frequently vilified or mocked as giving encouragement to the enemy or being out of touch with public opinion. She accepted the abuse and derision without complaint, but with an obsessive fear of insects and dirt, she was distressed at the sight of dog faeces pushed through her door. In the 1950s, she joined the Campaign for Nuclear Disarmament, challenging the incredulity and evil of a bomb that "could entail the wholesale destruction of millions".

Brittain's moral courage, compassion, and assured public speaking masked a shy, uncertain, and sensitive disposition. Rarely given to laughter - almost certainly the understandable consequence of too many appalling experiences - she contended with bouts of melancholy and, by her own admission, was "difficult to live with".

As her years increased and the great cause of peace she had championed still remained a dream, her faith in God grew stronger. In November, 1963, she wrote a prayer of thanksgiving and hope for all the "rich experience of my life in Thy beautiful world, the discipline of sorrow…and a world at peace in which to live and serve Thee". She had come to realise "that the years of frustration and grief and loss, of work and conflict and painful resurrection" would necessarily constitute the unfinished task of future generations. After a long illness precipitated by a fall, she died on Easter Sunday, 29th March, 1970, aged seventy six.

Brittain reminds us of the scriptural duty to 'hope against hope' (Romans 4. 18), to rise up again and again. For the sake of a peaceable kingdom, the seemingly impossible is always worth the struggle and the cost.

Rowan Williams
(1950 -)

"It should not be forgotten"

Rowan Williams was enthroned as the 104th Archbishop of Canterbury on 27th February, 2003. His enthronement sermon set out his priorities and concerns and attracted considerable attention. *The Times* newspaper printed it in full and even devoted a separate page to readers' questions concerning the future of the national Church he now led.

I know all this because of a culling of old press cuttings I undertook after Christmas that brought the carefully preserved sermon to my attention again. This one would escape the shredder. I read it carefully, using a highlighter on the parts that made me pause. I was left wondering why more than twenty years later, Williams's words continued to exercise and encourage me. I now realise it had something to do with Dr Johnson's wise observation that "in matters of religion, it is important not to be so much informed as reminded".

The strength and beauty of this sermon - the work of a gifted poet as well as a renowned theologian - amounts to more than the best thoughts in the best words (as Coleridge thought). It reveals a particular sensibility, one still shocked, and enthralled by the figure of Jesus and the ambiguous world into which he came to disclose its graced possibilities. Refusing the understandable option of a simple return to Christian basics in anxious times -

more 'full fat religion' or the making of disciples as the overarching purpose of the Church's remit - Williams goes further and deeper. He extends a deeply-felt and nuanced invitation to an inattentive culture and a fractious Church to think again about remarkable things. He asks the nation to remember why true religion might still matter in the market place and challenges the Church to recall how Christ, who is the secret of all hearts, comes to us as a stranger - "as one unknown" in Albert Schweitzer's words, but also as one who can be recognised as "more intimate to me than I myself".

To the lackadaisical, the bored or the politely agnostic who don't do religion and to those who are looking for something that might incline them to reconsider the Christian way, Williams points them to God. A God who is more than the projection of human needs and longings, and who cannot be confined to an idea, a theory or a set of propositions. A God who is "life, food, air for the stifled spirit and the beaten, despised, exploited body". He insists that the veracity of such a claim requires more by way of commitment than a casual nodding of the head or a tentative adherence to the cosy rituals of Christian believing: "It's only in the water that you can begin to swim." Switching metaphors, and continuing to address those who profess to have seen it all, who "know everything about bread, except that you're meant to eat it" - he invites them to taste and see that the truth of Christ is "indeed the bread of life". He makes a firm offer that is also generous and welcoming to the hesitant and uncommitted. It reminded me of W. H. Auden's observation "that love or truth in any serious sense, like orthodoxy, is a reticence".

Looking to the future and the kind of Church in which he will minister, Williams prays that it will possess courage aligned with an imagination fired by the vision of God, that leads to gratitude and joy. It will also "engage with passion in the world of our society and politics". Where there is human fragility and despair or the insults, injustices and violence "that blot out the divine image in our human relations" the Church should be ready to act, lament and warn of what the human future will represent if such warnings go unheeded.

Such a mission amounts to deep, difficult, and holy work, grounded in a constant readiness "to learn from the Bible and its shared life of prayer", and worship expressed through "noisy praise and silent adoration". The Church must learn to kneel again, to be silent in order to remember in love and contemplation the source of its life. This is the heart of its secret: a quiet confidence and strength that despite its manifest sins and imperfections - "the grime, the oil and dust of ages" - it is sustained by the Spirit that makes all things new and seeks to move it ever deeper into the mystery of Christ. It is in adoration and service that the Church will prove most authentically itself with "God in the midst of God's people…not any programme or manifesto, not any avalanche of projections."

The sermon ends with a telling personal story. About twelve years earlier during a visit to an Orthodox monastery, Williams went into an old chapel. On a simple altar was an unremarkable picture of Jesus that led to a moment of revelation:

"I saw as I had never seen the simple fact of Jesus at the heart of all our words and worship, behind the curtains of our anxieties and our theories, our struggles and our suspicion. Simply there; nothing anyone can do about it, there He is as He has promised to be till the world's end. Nothing of value happens in the Church that does not start from seeing Him simply there in our midst, suffering and transforming our human disaster." And He says to us: "If you don't know why this matters, look for someone who does - the child, the poor, the forgotten."

Here in all his immediacy, compassion and constancy, a Christ is set before us who brings us to our knees; who bids the Church cease its fruitless and obsessive chatter and look instead on Him. I remain grateful for the reminder.

Samuel Johnson. Unknown artist, no date
See page 164 image credits.

Samuel Johnson
(1709-1784)

To strive with difficulties and to conquer them

In 1752, two weeks after his wife's death, and stricken by remorse and grief, Samuel Johnson greeted the arrival of Francis Barber, a slave around ten years old from the sugar plantations of Jamaica. Brought to England two years earlier, it now occurred to Johnson's dear friend, Richard Bathurst, that the boy might be helpful to Johnson in his hour of need. In a way that few other Anglican Tories in the era of British slavery would have thought remotely conceivable, Johnson welcomed Francis into his home as companion and friend. Initially, the boy's domestic duties were light: preparing refreshment, waiting at table, answering the door, and keeping a watchful eye on Johnson's beloved cat, Hodge. As the months passed, Francis became a valued aid, distracting Johnson from the melancholia that had stalked him from his childhood, and proving invaluable as he struggled to compile what would prove to be the greatest achievement of his life as writer, essayist, critic, and biographer - *A Dictionary of the English Language.*

The task took almost ten years to complete and demanded all Johnson's massive erudition and resolve. As he amassed more than one hundred and sixteen thousand quotations, he began to doubt whether the project would ever be finished to his exacting lexicographical standards. There were also heated arguments with typesetters and bookbinders. All ended well and the publication of the dictionary made Johnson famous overnight: "I believe there is hardly a day in which there is not something about me in the newspapers." He was awarded an honorary Doctor of Laws degree by Oxford University, and after years of relative obscurity and hardship, the success of the dictionary made him financially secure. Johnson not only paid for Francis's education, but eventually left him the bulk of his estate. This magnanimous gesture set the seal on a delicate and sometimes exasperating relationship that to onlookers and friends most closely resembled that of father and son. Despite Francis's determination to seek employment and adventure elsewhere on at least two occasions over a period of twenty years, it proved a lasting and affectionate partnership, fuelled by Johnson's detestation of slavery when few opposed it.

Johnson's radical stance on slavery can still surprise. Until relatively recently, the pervasive myth of Dr Johnson as 'the great man of English letters' has been that of the backward-looking conservative, the fierce Tory defender of tradition, who resisted change or new ideas, especially if they threatened the established order. Johnson was unequivocal in his defence of the Church of England and its moral and spiritual role in the life of the nation and was gripped by a fear bordering on hatred of anarchy. But he was not an ideologue or stupid reactionary. In important respects he was both liberal and unorthodox, preferring his deep reading of human nature to conventional rules or received wisdom as the best and most reliable guide in human affairs. This led him to challenge the cruel and negative social and political attitudes of his day that denigrated black people as barbarous and savage - 'mischievous as monkeys and infinitely more dangerous'. The black British population at the time was about 15,000, most of whom were slaves. Their presence in towns or villages created unease with notable public voices declaring that within a few generations, they would become a source of contamination to English blood.

Johnson had no truck with such prejudices. On one occasion in Oxford in 1777, he caused considerable consternation in influential company by proposing a toast to "the next insurrection of the Negroes in the West Indies". This was not wine-fuelled or hypocritical table-talk on Johnson's part. Jamaica was Britain's most lucrative colony, generating astonishing wealth. Johnson, by contrast, knew it as a place of wickedness where on the sugar plantations there were twice as many deaths as births, and slaves typically survived seven years if they were not raped, flogged, hanged or burned alive beforehand. Like other early abolitionists, he paid close attention to reports of slave rebellions in the Caribbean, how violently they were suppressed, and how quickly they erupted again. An Anglican missionary observed that the first toy given to white children in Jamaica was a whip. The diary of a slave overseer, Thomas Thistlewood, recorded in unbearable and minute detail how he devised tortures and humiliations that forced some to defecate into other slaves' mouths or urinate in their eyes. After a deserved flogging, he would routinely pour lime juice into their wounds.

Against this inhumane reading of commodified human flesh that was seen as fit only for exploitation and subjugation, Johnson insisted that "no man is by nature the property of another" and that the real test of a civilised society was its treatment of the poor and excluded. He castigated the hypocrisy of the Americans who excelled at keeping slaves and yet issued the "loudest yelps for liberty". Because he believed in the uniformity of human nature and that therefore distinctions based on colour or race were morally abhorrent, it was right that Francis Barber should be redeemed from slavery and afforded the opportunity of education in England, just as the anonymous people in the streets should not be denied the chance of learning. In preference to the coffee houses of London where gentlemen discussed business and burgeoning colonial profits, Johnson favoured the taverns. There, he could converse with those who were failures or downtrodden, forget his innate sadness for a while, and entertain listeners with his wit and wisdom. When Johnson was told days before his death that he was going to be buried in Westminster Abbey, he replied directly, "place a stone over my grave that the remains may not be disturbed". The inscription placed over it stated simply his name, degree, date of death and age.

Willa Cather

(1873-1947)

"The immense design of things"

On Wednesday 7th June, 2023, six months before the 150th anniversary of her birth on 7th December, 1873, a sculpture of Willa Cather was dedicated and unveiled for the first time in the National Statuary Hall, Washington, DC. The base of the plinth is inscribed with a quotation from one of her acclaimed novels "*O Pioneers!*": "The history of every country begins in the heart of a man or woman". Above her name, in much larger letters, can be seen the solitary and imposing word, NEBRASKA. It was this vast territory on the Great Plains of America, and the courage and violence of frontier life, recorded and mythologised by Cather in her unique stories, that won her the Pulitzer Prize in 1922. In 1931, her face appeared on the front cover of *Time* magazine, confirming her place as a bright star in the American literary firmament.

In the Spring of 1883, when Cather was nine, she made the most significant journey of her life. Her family left the relative calm of Virginian society to escape the post-war South and immigrated to Nebraska to join grandparents and partake of cleaner air. With thousands of international settlers - Germans, French, Norwegians Czechs and Russians - and despite the threats of droughts, blizzards, and plagues of grasshoppers, they had been lured by the prospect of new beginnings and cheap farming land. On arrival, Cather believed she had come to the edge of the world.

For months she cried incessantly, and worried that she might die in a corn field, forgotten and alone. By the first Autumn however, this strange vista, ostensibly bereft of beauty, had claimed her heart and imagination. Even with the passage of time and long absences, she always knew it would be so.

Growing up in a town called Red Cloud, and inwardly somewhat confused and insecure, Cather occasionally dressed as a boy, cut her hair short, and referred to herself as 'William Cather Jr.' In the quietness of her attic room she read Tolstoy, Stevenson, and Bunyan under the bedsheets. Energetic, and something of an ambitious free spirit, she consorted with the 'Bohemians' constructing the railroad, delivered mail on a pony, helped out at a local pharmacy, and entertained dreams of becoming a doctor or surgeon. All the while, she was immersing herself in the lives of the immigrants as they battled heroically, and sometimes tragically, to adapt to the unyielding landscape and scarce resources. She marked their hopes and destinies and, years later, would make a compelling mosaic of their tales.

Before then there was the matter of her education and career. First, five college years in which her earlier inclination towards science gave way to classics and literature and a firm grounding in journalism. Then, a move to Pittsburgh as a journalist and arts reviewer, followed by a further stint as a school teacher, writing poetry and short stories in between lessons. In New York, and now in her thirties, she became managing editor of a successful magazine. The prestige was not enough to satisfy the writer in her. For several years she gave herself tirelessly to the demands of this new work but it was not her best self.

Approaching forty, Cather's Nebraskan past - the land itself, and its prairie dwellers, "none of whom had any appearance of permanence" - assumes a new perspective and purpose in her life. She becomes a novelist, a chronicler of great journeys, stoical endurance, and a landscape of severe and sometimes surreal wonder. She sets down the saving graces of domestic life and represents them as though seen for the first time: pots and pans, "little half-windows with white curtains, and pots of geraniums in the deep sills…and a pleasant smell of gingerbread baking".

In "*O Pioneers!*" Cather conjures a world far removed from sentimental rural nostalgia. She deals with the desires and fractures of human relationships that can never wholly satisfy, and the mortal questions touching life, birth, death and drama as the earth moves through its seasons. Darkness and promise permeate her vision as she charts the rising and setting of the sun, and the brief span allotted to the rugged figures reconfiguring the frontier with their backs and hands. In time, they will return to the earth, but not before they have witnessed moments of sudden transfigurations - "blond cornfields of red gold" and "the whole prairie like the bush that burned with fire and was not consumed". In *My Antonia*, young Jim Burden, the tutor of the heroine of the novel, sits in a garden where little red bugs with polished backs move around him. Nothing happens, yet he is entirely happy under the sky, "a part of something entire, whether it is sun and air, or goodness and knowledge".

Cather died, aged seventy four, on 24th April, 1947, and was buried in New Hampshire. The private life she had always desired, in which her Nebraska childhood had come to represent her best years, became more transparent with the first publication of her private letters in 2013. They reveal a warm, caring, and humorous disposition, at odds with her public demeanour that could appear aloof, judgemental, and somewhat detached. To one correspondent she writes: "Such a ravishing world, and such a short life in which to see it in." To another, she ends with, "May all the gold I ever dreamed of be yours."

Cather sought to live a Christian life. From childhood, church attendance remained important. Raised a Baptist, she was confirmed at the age of forty nine in the Episcopalian Church, and later became attracted to Catholicism. Her belief is declared resolutely in a private letter: "There is no God but one God, and Art is His revealer; that's my creed and I'll follow it to the end." At her life's close, and rendered frail through illness and grief, Cather still retained possession of "the precious, incommunicable past" with its beauty, darkness and promise, and ineffable moments of calm. Happiness for her resided in the possibility of being "dissolved into something complete and great" - appropriately, the words inscribed on her tombstone.

Richard Nixon. Office of the Vice President, Unknown photographer, between 1953 and circa 1961.

See page 164 image credits.

Richard Nixon
(1913-1994)

"Dick from the wrong side of town"

The 8th of August, 1974 proved a momentous day for millions of disenchanted and angry American voters. Following months of intensive investigations by the Washington Post, and a newly-established legal Office of Special Prosecutor, President Richard Nixon announced his resignation. The scandal of the Watergate affair involving burglary into the offices of his political opponents and the subsequent 'dirty tricks' and lies involved in the cover up that led to the White House, revealed that the 37th President of the United States was unworthy of its highest office and guilty of serious crimes.

Such accusations had long been familiar before Nixon's decision to resign. From the age of thirty three, fighting dirty had formed part of his controversial ascent to power. Rarely at ease with others or himself, power brokers and socialites mocked his upbringing and lack of charm. John F. Kennedy summed him up in two words: "No class."

Born in 1913, Nixon grew up in Los Angeles County. The son of a grocer, he rose daily at 4.30am to take vegetables to market before catching the school bus at 8.30am. Consistently top of his class, he was disliked by pupils who found him prickly and aggressive. At university, he appeared remote and socially awkward, a bookworm who gulped down his meals in the refectory so he could get back to the library to continue writing or reading. As his early career in law gave way to political ambitions, he did what was necessary to thwart or vanquish opponents in his path, in some cases making false accusations with the flimsiest of evidence. Later, he became a notable foe of communism, joining forces with the demagogue. Joseph McCarthy in his campaign against a 'creeping Communism' within the US government.

After failed bids for the presidency in 1960, and then for the governorship of California in 1962, Nixon worked assiduously to revive his career, calling on the "great Silent Majority" to resist the violence and excesses of the 1960s - the burning cities, the sexual revolution, and demands for rights for blacks and women - and promising to withdraw the American military from Vietnam. The strategy worked and in 1968 he was elected to the presidency. Vietnam soon became a yoke around his neck - an unwinnable conflict that led to further escalation and illegal bombings. His forced resignation in 1974, ended a career dogged by infamy and dodgy dealings seemingly leaving little by way of a worthwhile or lasting legacy.

Following a required statement of public contrition on Nixon's part, and in the face of mounting criticism, the incoming President, Gerald Ford, issued "a full, free and absolute pardon" to Nixon, who shortly afterwards almost died following surgery for a blood clot. After convalescence and a period of sustained reflection on his past, he sought to redeem his reputation, an undertaking still in progress at the time of his death twenty years later. At his funeral service, 50,000 people filed past his casket. In the presence of five former US Presidents, the evangelist Billy Graham praised Nixon as "one of the most misunderstood men, and, I think, one of the greatest men of the century".

The passage of time had tempered some of the animosity and disdain of the previous years. Many old enemies now conceded his gifts as an elder statesman, a supremely well-informed commentator on domestic and foreign affairs and an adviser to world leaders. A reappraisal of Nixon's former time in the White House also seemed just. This, after all, was the President who had opened up China to the Western world, established the Environmental Protection Agency and signed the Clean Air Act in 1970. He had also championed what became the National Endowments for the Arts and the Humanities, and increased federal funds for the racial integration of public schools. Those with long memories also recalled the dignity and unselfishness he displayed in not contesting the results of the 1960 presidential election, when many observers questioned whether President Kennedy had legally won the states of Illinois and Texas.

To the end of his life, Nixon retained a global vision of a better and more peaceful world. To this endeavour he brought a vast and deeply serious intellect nurtured by his passion for philosophy, biography and history and a resilience that overcame many personal and political obstacles. Flying back to California after his resignation, he reflected on the old Scots ballad that had seen him through griefs and dangers: "I am hurt, but I am not slain. I will rest and bleed awhile and then will fight again."

The clues to explaining Nixon's startling contradictions - the visionary yet vengeful leader who sought to overcome his faults even as he embraced the darker side of his nature, lie in his early life. Of crucial importance was the Quaker influence of his family, especially his mother, Hannah, commonly regarded as a quiet saint by her neighbours. Without ostentation or force, she introduced him to the moral precepts of the New Testament, the necessity of a silent grace before meals and Bible readings afterwards, regular church attendance on Sundays, and the striving for "peace at the centre" - an inner calm in the eye of the storm.

Even when Nixon failed to emulate her goodness and spirituality, Hannah remained the North Star of his morality and the animating spirit behind his ideals. Never far from his mind however, were two tragedies that had a profound impact on his character: the deaths of two brothers, one at the age of seven from encephalitis, and the other at twenty three of tuberculosis. In addition to his enduring grief, Nixon remained prey to deep-seated insecurities triggered by the grinding poverty of his childhood - he would always be 'Dick from the wrong side of town' - and the lifetime of social snubs and slights that exacerbated his resentments towards his critics, particularly the media and the liberal elites.

Nixon oscillated between bold and worthy initiatives that were shaped by religious convictions, and the tacky manoeuvres that generated the odium and shame leading to his downfall. It seems increasingly likely however, that history is already affording him the recognition and forgiveness that he desired and, in some measure, deserves.

Blaise Pascal
(1623-1662)

Scientist, saint and mystic

The relatively short life of Blaise Pascal, born in France on 19th June, 1623, chimes well with the sensibilities of our secular age. In part, it reflects a prevalent contemporary narrative of an individual achieving great things in the face of personal adversity before succumbing to an early death. Applause is often loudest for the brave and resolute who, against the odds and the unforgiving minutes, live out their truth tenaciously, before leaving a legacy for others to emulate or praise.

Pascal was a sickly child, who lost his mother at the age of three and suffered physical and mental pain for long periods throughout his life. By his early twenties, his food had to be liquefied to make digestion possible. In later years, his ailments grew worse: opinions on their causes included stomach cancer, tuberculosis or a brain lesion. He died at thirty nine in relative poverty on 19th August, 1662, and was buried in the parish church of Saint-Etienne-du-Mont, Paris, close by the Pantheon.

From childhood, and thanks largely to the home tuition provided by his father, Etienne, Pascal demonstrated an extraordinary aptitude for mathematics and science. Visitors to the family home marvelled at his precociousness. Years later, his peers would laud him as the 'Aristotle' of his age, immersed in experiments and inventions, including a calculating machine, and an early exponent of probability theory. In the last year of his life, he designed a transport system in Paris that, uniquely, assigned its profits to the needs of the poor. Some years before, along with friends, he had also initiated a scheme for reclaiming marshland in the Poitou Region for the material benefit of local residents. His genius and benevolence overcame formidable personal obstacles, inspired others - those closest to him came to view him as a saint - and improved the world.

There is, however, another narrative to explain why Pascal remains influential and read today when his inventions have been superseded and his good works have been largely forgotten. As a result of what he recorded as his two 'conversions', the Christianity that he had observed respectfully, like his father before him, gradually became a cause and passion. Without fully abandoning his scientific pursuits, he became involved in a religious revival within the Catholic Church which became known as Jansenism.

Jansenism had its roots in earlier Reformers and the thought of St Augustine. It emphasised the centrality of practical works of charity over pious exercises, the necessity of a deeper personal prayer life and an accompanying awareness of man's wretchedness and dependence on divine grace. The movement was declared to be heretical by the Catholic Church and faced an increasingly violent campaign. Pascal took sides and responded with eighteen polemical letters - the *Letters to a Provincial* - that brought him notoriety and acclaim. Admired for their literary style, they revealed a moralist with an intellectual passion for truth, and a readiness to confront the moral laxity and sophistry of the Jesuits, who were fuelling a bitter controversy that continued into the eighteenth century.

Pascal's second 'conversion' took place on the night of 23rd

November, 1654. Between 10.30pm and 12.30am, he underwent a mystical experience, a record of which survived in his own hand, and shaped decisively the course of his remaining years. After his death, the note that he always kept on his person was found sewn into the coat which he was wearing. It began: "Fire. God of Abraham, God of Isaac, not of the philosophers and scholars" and concluded with Psalm 119, v16: "I will not forget thy word. Amen." So it proved. From that night, Pascal resolved to give himself whole-heartedly to the service of God and others. This new calling included a defence of the Christian religion against its detractors. In particular, the free-thinkers and agnostics of fashionable society, who, Pascal believed, went through the motions of religion, but had no serious interest in truth or the proper moral strenuousness such practices required.

The intended *Apology for the Christian Religion* began to take shape around 1660, but Pascal's demise prevented its completion. What remained and subsequently published by his friends, came to be known as the *Pensées* - the notes, scattered papers, and various fragments that represented the recurring religious themes of Pascal's final years: the human predicament; the absolute centrality of Christ to the life of faith; the hiddenness of God; the truth of scripture, and the adequacy or fallacies of contrasting philosophical points of view.

For Pascal, true faith is inconceivable without virtue and the unending practice of charity. Civility and the refinement of personal manners and feeling will not suffice. Left to himself, "man is a monster, a chaos, a contradiction and a prodigy". Both fallen and wretched without God, he constitutes "the pride and refuse of the universe". On the one hand, capable of thought, reason and reflection and, ultimately, by the assistance of divine grace, a potential inheritor of eternal happiness. And, on the other, subject to meaninglessness, and forever captive to pride and desire. Salvation and ultimate happiness rest on rational human beings wagering with their lives on, what Pascal insisted, is the most important question of all: that God exists or does not.

A pale, sometimes icy tone, is evident in the *Pensées* that reflects the darker ruminations of Augustine concerning the attested deceits, evasions, and cruelties of the human heart. But as a spiritual classic, it represents much more than an accusatory wayside pulpit. Despite its fragmentary nature, and quite apart from the elegance and wisdom of its prose, and the memorable quotations that form part of contemporary intellectual discourse, it discloses an original mind, and, in a personal and moving way, the power and truth of the divine love that Pascal felt throughout his tribulations. A love that he wished others to share. The final words, fittingly, are his:

"So I hold out my arms to my *Redeemer*, who…has come to suffer and die for me on earth. By his grace, I await death in peace, in the hope of being eternally united to Him. Yet I live with joy, whether in the prosperity which it pleases Him to bestow upon me, or in the adversity which He sends for my good, and which He has taught me to bear by His example."

Denise Levertov
(1923-1997)

Poetry, protest and pilgrimage

Shortly before her death, aged seventy four, on the 10th December, 1997, and following a long terminal illness that she had kept from even close friends, Denise Levertov declined to be nominated as the next Poet Laureate of the United States. Concerned that the role might compromise her politics, she was, also in her view, an unsuitable candidate for other reasons. Most obviously, there was her increasing frailty. In addition, she had already been showered with fellowships, awards and prizes from various institutions and colleges in recognition of her work as a writer, activist, and poet of unusual distinction over several decades. It was the latter vocation that mattered most to her and for which she hoped to be remembered.

From a very early age, Levertov had envisaged her life's work as "a poet in the world". Her calling was that of a pilgrim dedicated to articulating her lived experience so that others might wake from their slumbers: "You know, I'm telling you, what I love best is life. I love life!" She was born in Ilford in 1923 to a Welsh mother, a singer and painter with an Evangelical faith, and a father, a Russian Jew who eventually became an Anglican priest and notable scholar. Both parents were political activists driven by a commitment to public service and a love of dance and literature. They schooled Levertov at home and books were everywhere. The poetry of Keats, Wordsworth, George Herbert, Rilke and

William Carlos Williams would all prove key to her artistic formation.

By early adolescence, Levertov had put organised religion to one side as too restrictive. It lacked the power of imagination that she believed was central to unlocking the meaning of the natural world and the great mystery that underpinned its turning. For a short time during World War II, she worked as a nurse in London tending the wounded and dying. The ending of hostilities in 1945 coincided with the publication of her first slim collection of poems. Increasingly restless however, and not terribly happy in a succession of fairly menial jobs in a dreary post-war England, Levertov sought new adventures. Europe beckoned, odd jobbing here and there in Holland and Paris; escapades sleeping in fields and haylofts, and an unwanted pregnancy that led to an abortion.

In 1948, after meeting and then marrying a young American writer, Mitchell Goodman, Levertov began a new life in New York. The literary scene was not to her liking in its self-importance and 'avant-garde' pretensions. In the decade and more that followed however, she found ample opportunities for poetry readings, teaching, and conferences on college campuses. More importantly, her poetic voice was attracting wider public recognition, even as she adjusted to the obligations of parenthood, following the birth of a son, Nikolai Gregor.

Levertov's poems came naturally, tumbling from her pen conveying her joy and sense of urgency as she "walked naked from the beginning, breathing in my life, breathing out poems, arrogant in innocence". Certain themes preoccupied her: the paradoxes and contradictions of a world containing hopes, promises and fears amidst the ever-present shadow of innocent suffering, cruelty, and death. Privately, she could be baffling, contrary, irksome and unbending to friends and detractors alike. She was also generous, supportive, funny, and vivacious; conscious of her beauty, yet also afraid of its fading. By way of reassurance and her felt need for the immersive experiences that her marriage lacked, she sought physical intimacy and delight in wider relationships that promised both.

By the 1970s, the American war in Vietnam and its aftermath had come to mark an anguished and prolonged phase in Levertov's life and art. News of the conflict dominated her waking hours and disturbed her rest. Horrified by the increasing casualties and deaths and the appalling level of attrition that she had witnessed first-hand on a visit to the war zone, her political engagement intensified. She could be found at pickets and protest marches or speaking at anti-war rallies, urging upon students "the necessity of revolution". She was arrested and monitored by the FBI. Critics called her naïve and dismissed her many protest poems as facile. Levertov thought otherwise, and railed against the easy acquiescence of contemporaries in the face of the morally indefensible: "O tolerance, what crimes have been committed in the name."

Turning sixty, Levertov found herself acknowledging a quiet but insistent move away from her lifelong agnosticism towards a deeper reckoning with Christianity. There was no moment of conversion; instead a growing acceptance on her part that religion, predicated on trust and hospitable to her questioning, was now integral to her 'faithful attention' to living out her chosen path.

Several collections of her poems reflected this transition. *Candles in Babylon* in 1982, Oblique Prayers in 1984, and *Breathing the Water* in 1987, led to her reception into the Roman Catholic Church in 1990. 'Annunciation' with its genuflection to Mary

- "Bravest of all humans, consent illumined her", remains a fine example of the lyricism of Levertov's later work.

Pilgrimages to Taize and Iona, and the newly-found influence of the writings of Julian of Norwich, all contributed to Levertov's renewed desire to be a better person, a more endearing, forgiving, and empathetic self. Her diary remained as full as ever, but now she felt a compulsion to speak of the inner spiritual life, her desire for, and gratitude towards God, and a heightened appreciation of those she had loved, but not always respected.

Levertov remained a pilgrim to the end, still in conversation with beliefs and traditions that spoke to her truth-seeking heart. Her funeral was held on the 26th December on a cold, grey day in Seattle. Around a hundred people gathered for the Requiem Mass, including Jews, Buddhists, artists and poets, and unbelievers. There were readings from Psalm 121, the prophet Isaiah, and the gospel of Matthew. Her laying to rest just a matter of hours after the Feast of the Nativity seemed entirely, if only fortuitously, in keeping with her poetic vision. The Incarnation had become for Levertov, the cornerstone of Christian believing. It disclosed the transcendent, abiding mercy of God in the very fabric of an ambiguous world, sustained "hour by hour, by a Lord Creator, Hallowed One".

Reinhold Niebuhr
(1892-1971)

Truth unvarnished

Reinhold Niebuhr, who died on 1st June, 1971, excelled in two callings. He was widely regarded as the most influential American theologian of the twentieth century and the greatest living political philosopher of his generation. With his gift for irony, and his awareness of the vagaries of history, he would not be surprised to learn that today, despite his acclaimed books, articles and sermons that elevated political and religious discourse and interrogated the powerful, he is known chiefly for one sentence that appears on page 705 of his *Major Works in Religion and Politics* in the Library of America:

"God, give us grace to accept with serenity the things that cannot be changed, courage to change the things that should be changed, and the wisdom to distinguish the one from the other."

The sentence with slight variations is known as the Serenity Prayer. Found everywhere on posters, plaques, cards, fridge magnets and placemats, it has also been adopted by Alcoholics Anonymous as an official meditation. Superficially, it reads like a plea to the Most High in time of personal need or trouble. But to know only a little about its author, is to realise that it is best understood as a summons to the moral clarity that makes possible a good and peaceable society ordered by a just politics. This endeavour constituted the abiding passion of Niebuhr's life and very public ministry.

Born in Missouri in 1892, and the son of a German Evangelical Pastor, Niebuhr was one of three siblings who distinguished themselves in the study, teaching, and practice of theology and social ethics. Following college, seminary, and Yale Divinity School, Niebuhr was ordained pastor in 1915 to serve at Bethel Evangelical church in Detroit, Michigan. In a city defined by the motor industry, industrial strife, racial and religious tensions, and the malign influence of white supremacists and the Ku Klux Klan, Niebuhr sided with the unions, spoke out against the KKK - "one of the worst specific social phenomena which the religious pride of a people has ever developed" - and over thirteen years increased his congregation from 66 to nearly 700. His influence and reputation grew. In 1928, impressed by the power of his preaching and writing, Union Theological Seminary, New York, appointed him Professor of Practical Theology. It proved a fortuitous move: a setting in the city that fed his capacity for hard thought and prayer, and the place where he fell in love with and married Ursula Keppel-Compton, a graduate student from Oxford.

For more than thirty years until his retirement from UTS in 1960, Niebuhr exercised a ministry that inspired students and clergy and wrote the texts that changed many lives beyond the seminary. *Moral Man and Immoral Society (1932)* made a deep impression on leading British politicians including Denis Healey and Tony Benn. The *Irony of American History (1953)* was described by one reviewer "as the most important book ever written on U.S. foreign policy." In a nation rife with racial inequality, Dr Martin Luther King Jr. drew on Niebuhr's social and ethical ideals and invited him to join the third Selma to Alabama March, in1965. A serious stroke prevented his attendance.

In the pulpit, Niebuhr frequently spoke without notes, engaging his listeners with his deep voice and the outstretched hand

and pointed finger of the biblical prophet. He attached the deepest significance to the Bible. From its pages, he derived his understanding of human nature in all its ambiguity. In *The Children of Light and the Children of Darkness (1944)* he wrote memorably, "Man's capacity for justice makes democracy possible; man's inclination to injustice makes democracy necessary."

Within the moral compass of scripture, and drawing on the thought of Augustine (especially his *City of God*), Calvin, and Karl Barth, Niebuhr formulated the principles and insights that refused easy answers from any quarter - religious or political - and called into question the moral obtuseness he identified within their domains. He challenged the crass optimism of liberals and their naïve thinking concerning the perfectibility of human beings and the assured inevitability of the nation's progress to a better future. He also took issue with conservatives who insisted on a literal interpretation of the Bible and promulgated what, in his view, amounted to an anaemic and attenuated version of 'true religion'. With regard to America's cherished identity as 'a city set upon a hill' blessed with a special providence, he rejected the myth of 'national innocence' in matters of international relations. There could be no such thing, he argued, on the part of a nation that had "killed red men, enslaved black men, and imported yellow men" to further its ambitions and prosperity.

Central to Niebuhr's thought was his 'Christian realism' which emphasised the sin of destructive pride that led to self-delusion in individuals and institutions, especially those making claims to perfection. He interpreted the religious life as one of perennial paradox: on the one hand, working unceasingly to transform society with faith in its graced but 'indeterminate possibilities' and, on the other, resisting the illusion that society could ever be perfected.

Now as then, Niebuhr's approach to matters of faith and morality offers no straightforward guide to action. The world is complex, "the mixture of good and bad in all human virtue" even more so. In such an unsettling dispensation, the Christian is required to act and choose, to embrace the path that as Niebuhr noted towards the end of his own fruitful yet demanding journey, was "full of grace and grief". Reading his work today in the light of our own fantasies and alarms suggests that we need his wisdom and unflinching self-scrutiny as much as ever.

Thomas Hardy. Unknown artist, circa 1912

See page 164 image credits.

Thomas Hardy
(1840-1928)

"Some blessed hope"

In 1891, as the novelist and poet, Thomas Hardy, was checking the proofs of *his* latest book, *Tess of the D'Urbevilles*, he paused to write a note of condolence to another writer, Henry Rider Haggard, whose ten year old son had just died. Expressing sympathy, Hardy continued: "Though to be candid, I think the death of a child is never really to be regretted, when one reflects on what he has escaped." As much as anything he wrote before or after, this terse and insensitive remark consolidated Hardy's reputation as a pessimist who viewed the world as 'a blighted star' and human life shot through with cruelty. His late novels divided families, readers, and critics. After reading *Tess*, Robert Louis Stevenson's verdict on the book was, in his own words, "spewed from my mouth". Four years later, the Bishop of Wakefield was so incensed by Hardy's relentlessly bleak novel, *Jude the Obscure*, that he threw the book on the fire and persuaded W.H. Smith to remove it from their circulation library. Unmoved by this ecclesiastical censure, the public devoured the tale and within three months of publication it had sold 20,000 copies.

Accounting for Hardy's belief in a malign or indifferent universe is one of the many paradoxes his life presents. He was a socialist of the champagne variety who eventually became rich and famous, travelled extensively, and enjoyed the delights and diversions that London and Paris had to offer. He was a driven, inattentive husband, locked in a childless and silently-decaying marriage who, after his first wife's death, produced astonishing poems of love and regret that are now regarded by his recent biographer, Claire Tomalin, as among "the most original elegies ever written".

Hardy was a believer and an unbeliever. An intermittent churchgoer throughout his life, he was well versed in the Prayer Book and the Psalms. He "cherished the memory of belief", the old parish rituals that endured through the flux of time - the "afternoons of drowsy calm…while we stood psalming there". In his youth, he contemplated the possibility of taking holy orders: a step too far, as he came to realise, and reserved for a quite different class of gentlemen. Still eager to learn and studying Greek in his spare time, he was influenced by the new thinking of radical philosophers and reformers such as Comte and Mill. Science engaged him, as did Darwin's revolutionary *Origin of Species*. Matthew Arnold's poem 'Dover Beach' with its poignant and melancholy evocation of a world of a faith that was passing away, reflected Hardy's own loss of religious certainties. On his death bed in the darkness of midwinter, he requested that the story of Christ's nativity should be read to him. Afterwards, he pointed that there was no evidence to support its veracity.

Hardy's own birth in 1840 was a distressing affair. He was so lifeless and tiny that the midwife thought he was dead and certainly did not expect him to survive. In early childhood he remained physically frail with a tendency towards solitude and a desire not to grow up. At twelve, along with a love of dancing, music and books, he developed a passion for languages and bought himself a Latin primer. Although he grew stronger, he endured bouts of depression that in later years caused him to go to bed "wishing to never see daylight again".

Hardy's childhood represents one possible source of his conflicted inner self. Although loved by his parents, they had been forced into marriage reluctantly, six months before his birth. His mother was intelligent and ambitious; she did not believe in marriage and had entertained a future other than the obscurity of rural domesticity. Looking back, it is feasible that Hardy came to see himself as both an unwanted child and an impediment to his mother's hopes of a more exciting and stimulating life elsewhere.

What is clear is the impact of failure and humiliation on his life before his talent was eventually recognised and rewarded. Along the way, he struggled with the rejection of manuscripts; the demand that they be revised or cut to avoid giving offence to prudish readers; the scorn and small-mindedness of reviewers and critics, and the sense, sometimes overwhelming, that like the anguished and unforgettable characters of his tragic stories, he was forever barred from advancement by a rigid class system, and the suffocating morality of his superiors. He never forgot the limitations of his humble beginnings, the years apprenticed to architects, when all the time he wanted to write, and did so - often in dingy lodgings beyond midnight. Many of his poems revisit the griefs and hurts of the past. The pain they inflicted never quite healed.

Hardy's wounds were largely concealed from his public. He rejected his reputation for pessimism, insisting that he was a realist with an unflinching eye for life's many ironies. In advanced old age, visitors found him affable and vigorous, still writing every day and continuing to read widely. To the end, he remained the ambivalent unbeliever, leaning on a coppice gate and hearing in the sound of an aging thrush, "some blessed hope, whereof he knew, and I was unaware". And in his most celebrated poem, 'The Oxen', published in *The Times* in 1915, when he was seventy five, he still yearned, as in the days of his childhood, to go to the crib on Christmas Eve and see the oxen kneel, "hoping it might be so".

Stewart Headlam
(1847-1924)

The roots of a radical

After more than fifty years of priestly ministry, Stewart Headlam achieved the rare distinction of being dismissed from all of the parishes in which he had served. In the process, he antagonised and frustrated bishops and incumbents, offended Victorian Christians, forged alliances with atheists and trade union leaders, and defended women's rights. He believed that the Eucharist was not only a revelation of God's beauty, but also a reminder that the divine kingdom would be established on earth and that "it would be as joyful as it would be just".

As a bohemian and aesthete, and a conscientious pastor, Headlam provoked anger and admiration in equal measure. He defended music hall ballerinas against the narrow sensibilities of religious bigots for whom exposed female flesh, could only ever be an invitation to lascivious desires, and enjoyed evenings in the Crown pub on the Charing Cross Road in the company of poets. He provided bail for drunks and, infamously, gave financial support to Oscar Wilde pending his trial and imprisonment.

In the East End, Headlam cared for the poor and uneducated. He nurtured hopes and aspirations, even as the clergy preached that life was a preparation for death, and that an alarming proportion of humanity would suffer the everlasting torments of hell. He rejected such bleak doctrines, insisting that all human beings were children of God and created for noble and beautiful things. Music hall dance could indeed provide intimations of the divine rather than lust. And so too could Shakespeare, Tennyson, history, and visits to the theatre. Such treasures were in keeping with the teaching of Jesus to live life more abundantly (John 10.10) and Headlam shared them with his parishioners.

Indirectly, the roots of this revolutionary creed were traceable to the pious evangelical home in the village of Wavertree, near Liverpool, where Headlam was born on 12th January, 1847. His father, Thomas, loved to argue with others concerning the religious controversies of the day and hoped that his son might come to share his opinions. Ever the contrarian, Headlam resisted. At Eton College and subsequently Cambridge University, he encountered the Christian Socialism of Frederick Denison Maurice. A Professor of Moral Philosophy, Maurice repudiated the doctrine of everlasting damnation, disliked intensely the uncritical worship of the Bible as if it were a divinely dictated text, and demanded that the Church should offer more than charity and the hope of a blessed hereafter. Its task was to teach that all were incorporated into the divine family and that cooperation rather than competition, was the basis of their common life. Christ was to be found everywhere - "in the shop and the marriage feast, wherever we go, whatever we are about".

Maurice's teaching, combined with the influential writings of the American political economist, Henry George, proved inspirational to Headlam and shaped his ministry. They also exposed him to accusations of heresy. Unrepentant, he resolved to preach Christianity as a liberating gospel that was humane, radical, open to questioning, and predicated on a trusting faith in "the self-sacrificing deliverer", Jesus Christ. In 1877, he founded the Guild of St. Matthew with the aim of studying social and political questions in order to bring about fundamental change in society. Socialists of every kind would be potential allies.

Despite its growing membership, the Guild's heady, if somewhat unfocussed political ambitions, made little practical headway in the established Church. Headlam was losing the trust of his bishop and therefore, the prospect of future paid employment. He had also separated secretly from his wife on discovering that she was a lesbian. The marriage was eventually dissolved. Critics spoke of him as 'somewhat deranged', an opinion shared by worshippers at a Maundy Thursday service in Westminster Abbey in 1881, as he preached on 'The Christian Communism of the Church of the Carpenter.' A few months later he was dismissed without compensation. He would survive on the private means inherited from his father, and the financial support of many well-wishers.

In the years that followed, Headlam continued to immerse himself in the work of educational and social reforms. He proved a dependable advocate for working class children and their teachers. He reminded the Church of its obligations to care for the poor and never lost the conviction that for all its imperfections, it remained a 'great institution' in need of renewal. Sadly, for him, the labouring masses he had reached out to felt no need to join the Church he loved or improve it. Headlam retained his passion for the ballet and the arts until his death on 18th November, 1924.

Prominent Christian Socialists attended his funeral, as did actors and actresses, Members of Parliament, county councillors, educationalists, and dancers. Shortly before his death, he had received a letter from the Archbishop of Canterbury, Randall Davidson. It concluded: "You at least, whatever may be said about the rest of us, have been consistent in your devotion to the cause or causes for which you care. God keep and bless you." In considerable pain, Headlam wrote a brief reply expressing his pleasure that "the old work has borne some fruit".

Headlam was a fallible prophet: inflexible, sometimes belligerent or myopic when wisdom or the readiness to concede another point of view was required, and worryingly vague as to how precisely the revolution would come about. But he was also principled, indefatigable, delightful company, and a friend to many, especially the forgotten. He saw more clearly than his bishops and opponents that the Christian gospel, by its very nature, was revolutionary in its social implications. To this day, the new 'incarnational' movement that he helped to establish continues to inspire Anglicans who 'seek the welfare of the city'. (Jeremiah 29.7).

Charles Dickens
(1812-1870)

"Much better to die, doing."

Death did not become Charles Dickens. When it came it was an affront to the fifty-eight years of his frenetic life in which he had entertained the masses, undertaken charitable works, championed great causes, and conducted a secret and passionate affair with the actress, Nelly Ternan, twenty seven years his junior. Shortly after their last meeting, he collapsed and died the next day, 9th June, 1870. Physically, he was a spent force, still capable of mesmerising his public audiences, but only with the assistance of opium and alcohol. A hurried funeral service was arranged for a few mourners and took place - against his wishes - in Westminster Abbey. Dickens' will stipulated there should be no pomp of any kind, and no public announcement of the time and place of his burial. The great bell was tolled; there was no singing or eulogy, just quiet organ music and the solemn reading of the burial service. Later, the grave was left open and thousands filed past to see his coffin and leave notes and flowers. Along with the legacy of his novels, the tears of mourners represented Dickens' best hope of immortality.

His religion, including a belief in a hereafter, was as complex as his life. For good reasons, we incline to see him in a Christian light: The festive season is unthinkable without *A Christmas Carol* and its message of hope and redemption. Tiny Tim does not die, Scrooge becomes a reformed character, and Bob Cratchit gets a long-overdue pay rise. The story ends with a benediction, "God bless us, everyone."

As a father, Dickens wrote the *Life of our Lord* principally for his children, as an encouragement that they should be merciful, kind, and forgiving. Apart from writing the great novels, and accepting the endless invitations to campaign against social evils or enjoy the conviviality of lunches, receptions, and the theatre, he was unstintingly generous to individuals and organisations. For twelve years, he gave his time and money to establish a refuge known as Urania Cottage that helped young women to turn their lives around. By his own estimation he was incapable of rest - "much better to die doing." The doing, in part at least, represented the outworking of his Christian principles.

If the example of Jesus inspired Dickens' philanthropy, churches frequently drew the savagery of his pen. For four years, possibly as a measure of his exasperation, he joined the Unitarians, who denied the divinity of Christ. He satirised the absurdities and hypocrisy of organised religion. Doctrinal divisions bored him, as did ecclesiastical history with its superstition and cruelties. Anglo-Catholic priests parading in fancy dress held no appeal. His main targets were ranting chapel preachers, and evangelicals pressurising Parliament to preserve the Lord's Day, thereby denying the wretched poor the few pleasures they had.

Dickens espoused a practical Christianity. The historical truth of the gospels, the saving power of the cross, and the hope of the resurrection mattered much less to him than the need to make life better for those who, through no fault of their own, had fallen short of the Victorian creed of respectability and self-improvement.

There was something indescribable about Dickens as he set about this work. The fusion of his genius and personal magnetism along with his passion for social reform proved irresistible. His recent biographer, A.N. Wilson notes: "It was only with partial irony that the New York Herald referred to his return to America to do the reading tour as the Second Coming." The ascription was exaggerated but, more importantly, it was misplaced.

For all the laudable aspects of Dickens' gospel, in his private and family life he was frequently neither benign nor loving, and lacked the milk of human kindness he commended to others. As he grew older, he became less liberal in his attitude towards penal reform and poverty and failed to acknowledge the exemplary work among the poor by the chapels and clergy he held in disdain. His long standing affair with Nelly Ternan was only possible through meticulous subterfuge. His deplorable treatment of his wife Kate, who had raised their ten children, included her public humiliation by Dickens, his obsessive control of her domestic duties and expenditure, his disrespectful remarks to others concerning her character and appearance, and his attempt to have her removed to an asylum when there was no evidence of her being insane. All this caused incalculable pain and misery to the children. On one occasion, Dickens confessed his failures as a father to his daughter, Katey. Much later, she recorded that she knew things about her father's character that no one else knew: "He was not a good man, but he was not a fast man, he was wonderful!"

Outside the unhappy and vindictive atmosphere of the household, Dickens was, indeed, wonderful - wherever he went "a sort of brilliance entered the room". This leaves unexplained his callousness and indifference towards those closest to him or for that matter his lack of self-awareness that such behaviour was quite inimical to the precepts of Jesus that he commended to his children. We are left with a mystery: the bad, unfaithful husband

and inattentive father, who noticed the small, inconsequential lives on the streets of London, and immortalised them in his books. The 'inimitable' Dickens whose energy and drives contributed so much to Christianity and the common good, yet in the end destroyed him.

Thomas Müntzer
(1489-1525)

The poor shall not be forgotten

Outside of academic circles, sharing a research interest in the Reformation, relatively few readers will be aware that 2025 marks the 500th anniversary of the German Peasants' War. The largest popular uprising in Western Europe prior to the French Revolution, it grew in successive waves at the height of the Reformation, terrifying feudal powers and costing up to a hundred thousand lives. Its causes remain contested - a succession of bad harvests, the avarice of landowners, the indolence and corruption of the Church, and the desperation of ordinary people to ameliorate the harshness and injustice that diminished their lives and freedoms all played a part.

Peasant leaders justified insurrection by appealing to 'God's law', first, by drawing on their version of Luther's teaching concerning grace and salvation, and later insisting that serfdom was incompatible with the word of God. Twelve Articles of March, 1525, drafted in the southern town of Memmingen, were littered with scriptural references. Peasants were no longer to be regarded as mere chattels because "Christ has redeemed and bought us all by the shedding of his precious blood". Dismayed and angered by the destruction and killings precipitated by the uprising, Luther condemned the rebellion's leaders for their abuse of the Bible in support of their cause and was deeply perturbed by their rejection of those set above them who, based on his reading of Romans

13, exercised divine authority. Denouncing the Memmingen Articles as 'the Devil's work', he penned a notorious tract, *Against the Robbing and Murdering Hordes of Peasants*. In it he called on the German princes to restore secular authority and to "stab, smite, strangle" opponents without mercy.

One peasant leader in particular who had come to represent a serious threat to vested interests, was a passionate and often penniless itinerant preacher named Thomas Müntzer. Born in 1489, the son of a coin maker and educated at the universities of Leipzig and Frankfurt, Müntzer's reputation as a militant revolutionary, advocating riots and bloodshed, grew as he preached in towns and cities in Saxony and Bohemia. Frequently offending local authorities and subsequently being expelled by them, he castigated princes as "a miserable, wretched sack of maggots". Rejecting Luther as "Doctor Liar" and resorting to course and vituperative language employed by Luther himself in his denunciations of the late medieval Papacy, Müntzer wrote: "I shit on your Scripture and Bible and Christ unless you have the knowledge and spirit of God."

Müntzer's life ended violently when he stood with 6,000 peasants massacred by superior troops at the Battle of Frankenhausen on 14th and 15th May, 1525. Following torture with thumbscrews and a forced confession, he was executed. His head was placed on a pole as the severest warning to others entertaining a new social order and a reminder that this was how God punished disobedience. The authorities expected that Müntzer would soon be forgotten, afforded only the legacy of a heretical loser. In an obituary notice, Luther described him as "that murderous and bloodthirsty prophet" who, boasting that "God spoke and acted through him", now lay dead, visibly forsaken by God, along with the thousands who had perished in the mud of Frankenhausen.

The mud, so to speak, stuck. In a matter of years, Müntzer's name and influence largely waned. The Anabaptist movement initially drew inspiration from his teachings as it spread across Germany and the Netherlands following the peasants' brutal suppression, but a mendacious myth devised by Müntzer's opponents, ensured that posterity would remember him, if at all, as a failed rebel, an apostate concerning true religion, and a threat to a political dispensation ordained by God.

The myth approximated to a character assassination, but it did contain an important truth: Müntzer did believe that he was a prophet of God - a new Moses or Elijah, who as part of God's Elect (his predestined chosen people) was living in the last days, in order to summons society to repentance and a greater conformity to God's will. To this endeavour, Müntzer brought his deep knowledge of the Bible as well as the significant theological writings of the Middle Ages. A professed intellectual, he loathed academics cloistered in privileged surroundings, content on the one hand with a venal ruling class and, on the other, seemingly indifferent to the paucity of peasants' tenuous lives. Anticipating Luther, he was a reformer of German liturgical worship and texts (most notably the Psalms), insisting that only German be spoken and that whole chapters of the epistles and gospels be read so that people were edified spiritually and liberated from the mystifying priestly mumblings and incantations of the Latin Mass. A mystic who believed that God spoke immediately in dreams and visions, he encouraged his followers in the expectation that God would write directly in their hearts "with His living finger". Without such experience, Scripture was merely a record of God's former dealings with his people rather than the revelation of his ultimate and unchanging "word". Individual suffering, mental and physical, was an inevitable and indispensable feature of the habitation of the Elect "for only then can someone who has been tested preach God's name". Müntzer's own afflictions and manner of death served to confirm in his own experience the veracity of this central aspect of his radical teachings.

Müntzer's life and thought merit serious and sympathetic attention. As Professor Bridget Heal pointed out in a recent review of a new biography, his story signifies "the extraordinary dynamism and fervour of the early years of the German Reformation". No less, however, it confirms the place of the emotions in the religious life. The cause of God's truth extends beyond the uncritical acceptance of doctrines or texts and demands both the assent of the heart and the impulse of justice. Luther inveighed against a Church that had abandoned the narrow way of Christ for worldly power and wealth, but was unwilling to recognise that the forced resignation of the lowly and meek to God's will, contained within it the seeds of revenge and revolution. Müntzer perceived that a truer and more radical reformation of society and manners also required a readiness to challenge secular authority and social injustice in the name of God and for the sake of the perilous poor.

Postscript

"Spiritual gold reserves"

A simple drawing in a recent edition of *The Spectator* caught my attention. It depicts a tiny congregation huddled together in equally sparse pews. The roof and parts of the walls of the church are missing and the stonework of the entrance door is crumbling. The faithful shelter under umbrellas as rain falls from a grey sky; surrounding them is a landscape of winter trees bearing barren branches. Two indistinct figures stand outside the tottering façade. They appear to be a parent and young person peering in, but somewhat uncertain about entering. In the foreground a black crow perches impassively on a fence.

At first glance the picture appears a warning or lament, perhaps even a farewell. An acknowledgement of the corrosion of time and trust; a parting of the ways, and a national Church shorn of credibility and integrity through a crisis of leadership spanning decades. Looked at more closely however, the drawing invites more than an epitaph. It draws the eye to the two or three barely visible worshippers who have assembled in a once holy place where, in T. S. Eliot's memorable phrase, "prayer has been valid". They have turned up as their forebears did and perhaps prayed much, even on the rainiest of days when the harvest of souls was meagre. They constitute the laity that maintain the Church in truth when its leaders dissemble or fail. Such was the conviction of no less a prelate than St. John Henry Newman.

In 1859, Newman penned his last article as editor of *The Rambler*, a post he had held for a short time and only after much persuasion and prayer. In this role his aim was to encourage serious thinking on the part of the then torpid Catholic hierarchy in England with regard to modern science and scholarship, and, even more controversially, the proper and dignified function of the laity in the Church. His measured thoughts fared badly. Summoned to a private meeting with his bishop, Newman was asked dismissively "Who are the laity?" In a memorable reply, he retorted "that the Church would look foolish without them".

His final editorial contribution underpinned this claim by means of an extended essay that caused much controversy at the time and was not reprinted or published in England until 1961. *In Consulting the Faithful in Matters of Doctrine*, Newman argued that if the world was to know something of the truths of 'Christ, the Great Teacher', it should look not only to its bishops, but also the beliefs and practices of the ordinary, unremarked faithful who were equally custodians and stewards of the 'deposit of faith'. From his immersive studies of the early centuries of the Church, marked by internal theological hatreds and violent disagreements, he had come to disquieting conclusions. When bishops had contradicted one another on fundamental matters of doctrine and the weakness, prevarications and misguidance of a divided hierarchy threatened to eclipse the light of Christ, it was the body of the laity that clung to the narrow way. What they firmly believed, sustained and illuminated their living, suffering, and dying.

The essay was never intended as a rebuke to the Church leaders of his day. Newman believed that the truth of Christ was mediated in various ways including the utterances of the episcopacy. But he also placed considerable stress on the *consensus fidelium*, the consent and attested witness of the faithful. Like the first apostles, they too had received and were guided by the Holy Spirit. What the Church was therefore in its very essence, its nature, form and possible futures, was shaped in part by the devotion and spiritual integrity that started from below within the body of believers. The laity were to be listened to and consulted not simply because they too had their story, but rather that their collective experience reflected their graced instinct of the faith (*sensus fidei*). Together with priests and bishops they shared a common mission and a call to holiness.

Newman's prescience remains timely and even more urgent as the national Church looks to appoint a new Archbishop. It should acknowledge, celebrate and draw on "the spiritual gold reserves" (interestingly, a term first coined by the late Chief Rabbi, Jonathan Sacks) of faithful congregations and prayerful souls, however small. We may choose to call them little platoons, quietly alert and active in countless parishes or communities of character shaped by an inner voice insisting on the truth above everything. They are the Church, its treasures from below, indifferent in the best sense to the warring motions of a General Synod or the larger institutional preoccupation with numerical decline. If we are to think and pray wisely concerning the future mission of Christianity to a disenchanted nation, we shall hardly see the road ahead if we fail to pay attention where it matters. In the first instance, as Newman insists, to be encouraged by those who have gone before us as the people of God, and then to value those who continue to make Christ known in their localities through unfaltering prayer, fidelity, and service.

Suggested Further Reading
(In profile order)

Gardner, K. J,	*Betjeman and the Anglican Imagination,* (SPCK, 2010)
Gardner, K. J,	*Faith and Doubt of John Betjeman,* (Continuum, 2005)
Wilson, A. N,	*Betjeman,* (London: Hutchinson, 2006)
Bew, J,	*Citizen Clem: A Biography of Attlee,* (Riverrun, 2016)
Hennessey, P,	*Never Again: Britain,* 1945-51, (Penguin, 2006)
Dillard, A,	*Pilgrim at Tinker Creek,* (Canterbury Press, 2011)
Dillard, A,	*An American Childhood,* (Harper & Row, 1987)
Solzhenitsyn, A,	*The Gulag Archipelago,* (Vintage Classics, 2018)
Vanstone, W. H,	*Love's EndReavour, Love's Expense,* (DLT, 1998)
Healey, E,	*Emma Darwin,* (Headline Publishing, 2001)
Blake, R,	*Disraeli,* (Faber & Faber, 2010)
Spencer, S,	*Christ in All Things: William Temple and His Writings,* (Canterbury Press, 2015)

Gordimer, N, *Telling Times: Writing & Living, 1954-2008*, (W.W. Norton, 2010)

Brater, E, *The Essential Samuel Beckett: An Illustrated Biography*, (Thames & Hudson, 2003)

Webster, J, *The Cambridge Companion to Karl Barth*, (Cambridge University Press, 2000)

Norris, K, *Dakota: A Spiritual Geography*, (Houghton Mifflin, 1993)

Monk, R, *Inside the Centre: The Life of J. Robert Oppenheimer*, (Jonathan Cape, 2012)

Norman, J, *Adam Smith: What He Thought and Why it Matters*, (Penguin, 2019)

Healey, E, *Lady Unknown: The Life of Angela Burdett-Coutts*, (Sidgwick & Jackson, 1978)

Brown, G, *My Life, Our Times*, (Bodley Head, 2017)

MacMillan, J, *A Scots Song: A Life of Music*, (Birlinn Ltd, 2019)

Dudgeon, P, *Lifting the Veil: The Biography of Sir John Tavener*, (Portrait, 2003)

Jenkins, K, *Still With The Music: My Autobiography*, (Elliott & Thompson, 2015)

Berry, P, *Vera Brittain: A Life*, (Virago Press, 2001)

Brittain, V, *Testament of Youth*, (Virago Press, 1979)

Shortt, R,	*Rowan Williams: An Introduction*, (DLT, 2003)
Wain, J,	*Samuel Johnson*, (Macmillan, 1980)
Martin, P,	*Samuel Johnson: A Biography*, (Weidenfeld & Nicolson, 2008)
Lee, H,	*Willa Cather: A Life Saved Up*, (Virago Press, 1997)
Cather, W,	*Death Comes for the Archbishop*, (Penguin, 2003)
Perlstein, R,	*Nixonland: The Rise of a President and the Fracturing of America*, (Scrivener, 2008)
Aitken, J,	*Nixon: A Life*, (Weidenfeld & Nicolson, 1993)
Krailsheimer, A. J,	*Pascal*, (OUP, 1980)
Pascal, B,	*Pensées*, (Lector House Publishing, no date)
Greene, D,	*Denise Levertov: A Poet's Life*, (First Illinois, 2014)
Fox, R. W,	*Reinhold Niebuhr*, (Cornell University Press, 1997)
Tomalin, C,	*Thomas Hardy: The Time Torn-Man*, (Viking, 2006)
Orens, J. R,	*Stewart Headlam's Radical Anglicanism: The Mass, The Masses, and the Music Hall*, (University of Illinois Press, 2003)

Tomalin, C, *Charles Dickens: A Life*, (Viking, 2011)

Wilson, A. N, *The Mystery of Charles Dickens,* (Atlantic Books, 2020)

Drummond, A, *The Dreadful History and Judgement of God on Thomas Müntzer: The Life and Times of an Early German Revolutionary*, (Verso, 2024)

Image Credits
(In order of appearance)

John Betjeman. Statue created by Christoph Braun, 2012.
No sources information. Copyright Public Domain
https://commons.wikimedia.org/wiki/File:John_Betjeman,_London,_England,_GB,_IMG_4991_edit.jpg

Clement Attlee. Unknown photographer, 1945.
Source https://library.flinders.edu.au/images/ims/?id=31560859694&size=thumb3
Copyright Public Domain
https://commons.wikimedia.org/wiki/File:Clement_Attlee_portrait.jpg

Emma Darwin. Painted by George Richmond, 1840.
No source information. Copyright Public Domain
https://commons.wikimedia.org/wiki/File:Emma_Darwin.jpg

Samuel Beckett. Photograph taken by Roger Pic, 1977.
Source Bibliotheque nationale de France. Copyright Public Domain
https://commons.wikimedia.org/wiki/File:Samuel_Beckett,_Pic,_1_bw.jpg

Robert Oppenheimer. Department of Energy, Office of Public Affairs. Circa 1944.
Source taken from a Los Alamos publication (Los Alamos: Beginning of an era 1943-1945, Los Alamos Scientific Laboratory, 1986) Copyright Public Domain
https://commons.wikimedia.org/wiki/File:JROppenheimer-LosAlamos.jpg?uselang=en#Licensing

Unless otherwise indicated, this information has been authored by an employee or employees of the Los Alamos National Security, LLC (LANS), operator of the Los Alamos National Laboratory under Contract No. DE-AC52-06NA25396 with the U.S. Department of Energy. The U.S. Government has rights to use, reproduce, and distribute this information. The public may copy and use this information without charge, provided that this Notice and any statement of authorship are reproduced on all copies. Neither the Government nor LANS makes any warranty, express or implied, or assumes any liability or responsibility for the use of this information.

Gordon Brown. Photograph taken by Eddie Vanderwalt, 2007.
Source Gordon Brown Flickr account
https://www.flickr.com/photos/24921807@N05/28235954926/ Copyright Public Domain https://commons.wikimedia.org/wiki/File:Gordon_Brown_(28235954926).jpg

Samuel Johnson. Unknown artist, no date.
Source Duyckinick, Evert A. Portrait Gallery of Eminent Men and Women in Europe and America. New York: Johnson, Wilson & Company, 1873. p. 5 Copyright Public Domain https://commons.wikimedia.org/wiki/File:Samuel_Johnson_EMWEA.jpg

Richard Nixon. Office of the Vice President, Unknown photographer, between 1953 and circa 1961.
Source US National Archives. Copyright Public Domain
https://catalog.archives.gov/id/16916176
https://commons.wikimedia.org/wiki/File:Richard_Nixon_official_portrait_as_Vice_President.tiff?uselang=en

Thomas Hardy. Unknown artist, circa 1912.
Source The World's Work, 1912: https://archive.org/stream/worldswork24gard#page/376/mode/2up Copyright Public Domain
https://commons.wikimedia.org/wiki/File:Portrait_of_Thomas_Hardy.jpg